SCRIPTWRITING

SCRIPTWRITING

UEA MA
Creative Writing Anthologies
2019

CONTENTS

JAMES MCDERMOTT	Foreword	VII
STEVE WATERS	Introduction	IX
DIMITRA BARLA	Maternity Ward	2
TAYLOR BEIDLER	Coke Burns Brightest on the Allegheny	14
MAGDALENE BIRD	Baby Blue	24
ALICE COULTHARD	Afterbirth	38
JACK MARCUS FITCH	A Life in the West	48
NATALIE FROOME	Influence	58
SAI HAVAL	A Memory of a Cupboard	70
JESSIE LOCKIE	Mould	82
JAMES PICKTHALL	Entropy	94
FIONA SANGSTER	The Organ Donor	104
KATIE STOCKTON	Colloquium	114
	Acknowledgements	125

JAMES MCDERMOTT
Foreword

I always wanted to write plays but I never thought I could as the plays I had to study at school were never about or by queer people like me and they were all set in London or America as opposed to Lincolnshire and Norfolk where I was brought up.

In sixth form, I expressed this to my media teacher who then gave me Jonathan Harvey's collected plays. Jonathan's queer plays set in Liverpool showed me that plays can be about anything, by anyone and be set anywhere. They inspired me to start writing the plays I wanted to see in the world.

So I could learn how best to write my plays, my media teacher encouraged me to study scriptwriting at university. I dismissed this suggestion, assuming that playwriting couldn't be taught. My media teacher told me that if you want to be a pianist, you can't compose a symphony without first learning musical chords. If I wanted to be a playwright, I couldn't write a good play without first learning about dramatic structure and studying the work of great playwrights. I applied to study for a BA in Scriptwriting at UEA.

During my BA, I was taught tools to help me generate stories, create characters, write dialogue and structure scripts. I read many different plays broadening my empathy as a human. My reading as a student and my awareness as a writer taught me that as a playwright I could indeed write about anything.

At the end of my BA, tutors guided me through the writing of *Rubber Ring*, my one man comedy play about a confused Norfolk teenager struggling with sexual and regional identity. *Rubber Ring* went on to tour the country, be published by Samuel French, and I am currently adapting it for TV. I don't believe the play would have been written without tutors at UEA teaching me the tools I needed to write it and supporting me through the process of penning it.

I then received a bursary to study for an MA in Scriptwriting at UEA. On that course, I learnt about form and how the content of your play can be reflected in the shape of your play. I learnt that the spelling of 'playwright' reveals what the job of the playwright is: to wrought the verbal, physical, and psychological games human beings play with each other as they try and win something. I learnt that rewriting is the process of trying to find the play you want to write behind the play you've written.

Having explored my own identity in my BA dissertation play *Rubber Ring*, tutors encouraged me to write a bigger, bolder play about sexuality and regional identity for my MA dissertation play. I wrote *Time and Tide*, a five-act four-hander about the intergenerational staff of a Cromer caff learning to live with and love each other. *Time and Tide* is having a London production in 2020 and I am currently adapting it for TV. Again, this play wouldn't have been written without tutors encouraging me as much as they did on the MA.

Everything I learnt during my time at UEA has affected everything I've written and everyone I've taught since graduating. Tutors' advice always to strive to write bigger, bolder plays inspired me to write *Street Life*, a verbatim play commissioned by Norwich Theatre Royal which explored homelessness in Norfolk, and *CAMP!*, a cabaret show co-commissioned by Norwich Theatre Royal and Norwich Arts Centre which makes a song and dance about mainstream media's silence on the anti-gay purges in Chechnya. What I learnt on the course underpins my creative writing teaching in schools and theatres across the county.

I now agree with what my media teacher told me about writing when I was eighteen. If you want to be a good scriptwriter, it's wise to learn your craft by studying the plays of others alongside workshopping your own plays with other developing writers. The MA in Scriptwriting course at UEA gave me the space, time and support to do this and every year gives the space, time and support to a new generation of scriptwriters to do this, too.

STEVE WATERS
Introduction

As a veteran writer and teacher of writers I like to read the runes nascent in the work of our talented cohort here at UEA. How does the class of 2018/19 speak of and to the increasingly unpredictable world? The actor and dramatist Anna Deveare Smith eloquently claims the task of the writer is to, 'suggest, imagine and suppose'; any act of writing dares to offer a view of and on the world. And the short dramas that follow add up to a kaleidoscopic vantage point that casts modern life in a radical new light.

What a riot of forms that these global writers draw on! Sai Haval brings from India a tradition of humane and detailed observation; her short 'A Memory of a Cupboard' exemplifies this approach in its subtle account of ageing conceived in highly visual terms. Taylor Beidler, from the US, draws down a different movie heritage in 'Coke Burns Brighter on the Allegheny', a gritty chilly drama of post-industrial decline, with kinetic images of seriously bad parenting – whilst from Greece, Dimitra Barla offers an elegant and theatrical dissection of three sisters in present and past as they await another addition to their tribe.

Is it surprising that birth, death and family predominate? The diversity of such age-old themes might be reimagined and can be seen in the gap between Alice Coulthard's 'Afterbirth', a terrifying and visceral mapping of the trauma of birth and after, and Magdalene Bird's 'Baby Blue', which plunges us into the minds of her PND-stricken couple through artfully expressionist radio technique. That same psychological approach informs the haunting grief-stricken imagery of Jessie Lockie's 'Mould', where memory and reality meld. Elsewhere, Fiona Sangster fearlessly refreshes the cop drama through the sheer panache of her whiplash images and observant humane gaze and Jack Marcus Fitch reboots the Western in 'A Life in the West' as, after witnessing her father's death, a traumatised daughter grows up to become a vengeful gunslinger.

If that all seems rather bleak, there's plenty of laughs here too; 'Influence', Natalie Froome's wickedly observant flatshare satire, dissects Shoreditch hipsters with infectious glee. More disturbingly, Katie Stockton offers up an outrageously funny anatomy of the snobbish contortions of an Oxbridge admissions process; whilst James Pickthall's 'Entropy' is a wry road movie for radio, centring on a gay couple trying to reboot their relationship.

In the pages that follow, you will meet eleven young writers all set to reshape the world of drama, their short scripts advance warning of stories to come. This anthology suggests the future of drama is in safe hands whatever happens to the world beyond the stage or screen.

SCRIPTWRITING

DIMITRA BARLA

Dimitra Barla is a scriptwriter and actor. She is a graduate of East 15 Acting School and the Media and Communication Department of the University of Athens. Her work has been presented at the Wallace Collection, the Camden Fringe Festival, the Hellenic Centre, the Vault Theatre Festival and Everyman Cinemas.

MATERNITY WARD
(a short play in two scenes)

SCENE 1

The waiting area of a Maternity Ward. Dora Sienna sits on a chair, looking over some papers. She's in her late 30s and dressed in a suit. On the chair next to her, there's a briefcase and a lady's coat. On a third chair there's a jacket and a backpack.

Ella Sienna enters holding two cups of warm refreshments. She's in her early 30s, dressed casually. She doesn't sit down.

>   ELLA
> They didn't have Earl Grey, just yellow tea.
> And no soy milk either. I put in some normal,
> the cow one.

>   DORA
> It's fine, thank you. You're having coffee?

>   ELLA
> Yes.

>   DORA
> How many have you had?

>   ELLA
> Since this morning or this afternoon?

>   DORA
> You drink too much coffee.

Pause

>   ELLA
> Anyone come out?

Dora nods no.

>   ELLA
> Any sign from Marcus?

>   DORA
> No, sadly, none.

ELLA
Will you ring him?

DORA
Again?

ELLA
You know he won't return my calls!

DORA
You're exaggerating.

Dora takes her phone out and dials a number. No answer. She leaves a voicemail.

DORA
(on the phone)
Hi Marcus, it's Dora again. Please ring me as soon as possible. I've got news that can't be shared in a voicemail. Thank you and I hope you're well.

ELLA
I cannot believe the guy.

DORA
It's five AM in China. He's probably asleep.

ELLA
Would you be so gracious, I wonder, if Theo did that to you? I can think of at least a hundred different ways you would torture him to his dying breath.

DORA
Marcus isn't doing anything harmful to Francine. Were he actually in the country, it would be different. Given the situation, him not knowing changes absolutely nothing.

ELLA
Hear hear, your honour and well-respected court!

DORA
You're being funny.

ELLA
If only it'd been Theo!

DORA
Will you please stop it with Theo! Anyway, we're here and we're enough.

Pause. Ella sits.

ELLA
How much longer do you think it's going to take?

DORA
I don't know.

ELLA
Mum said it took fifteen hours for you to pop out.

DORA
But only seven for you.

ELLA
And two for Francine.

ELLA/DORA
(imitating their mother)
'Most caring child!'

ELLA
I always found it odd that Francine came out faster than me, I'm the youngest.

DORA
And the most impatient.

ELLA
You're the stubborn-est.

DORA
I'm the wisest.

Pause. Ella stands up.

ELLA
I wouldn't say no to another cuppa.

DORA
(giving Ella her cup)
Me neither.

ELLA
I just went.

DORA
You're already on your feet.

ELLA
It's your turn.

DORA
Don't be so childish.
(imitating Ella)
'Your turn'.

Ella sits down. She takes a script out of her backpack. Dora takes a bottle of water out of her bag and drinks. Pause.

DORA
What are you reading?

ELLA
I'm studying.

DORA
What are you studying?

ELLA
My sides. An audition. For a film.

DORA
Does it pay?

ELLA
Yes.

DORA
Is it a good part?

ELLA
Yes.

DORA
How many actresses are they seeing for it?

Ella puts the script away.

ELLA
It's two pounds fifty for the tea and another two fifty for the coffee. That's five pounds in total. It's the twenty-fourth of the month, I'm not getting paid until the thirty-first, and I'm left with fourty-seven pounds and seventy-five pence in my bank account to eat and travel. So sure, I'm childish, whatever. I don't expect you to understand.

DORA
I don't understand? I support you any way I can.

ELLA
Thanks for the charity.

DORA
Don't take your frustrations out on me. These are all your choices.

ELLA
Right! Shitty day job, tiny flat and — and being alone for the past four years! My choices! Can't you find anything new to say?

DORA
Yes, Ella, they are! You're so focused on your acting you're pushing people away.

ELLA
I'm pushing people away? I'm pushing people away? I don't remember being the one calling in the middle of the night all hysterical because—

DORA
Because what? Say it! That was very hurtful.

ELLA
I'm sorry. I'm so stupid. I'm sorry, please don't cry. I'm so stupid.

DORA
But you're right. I completely... fucked up.

ELLA
Don't be so hard on yourself. It always takes two to tango. After all, buying a house is one of the most stressful things for any couple.

DORA
Theo's bloody fixation with the countryside! I can't live in the middle of nowhere, I want to be in the city.

ELLA
We're city girls!

DORA
And I have been the one putting in more money.

ELLA
Law does put more in the privy purse than landscape gardening!

DORA
He looked so miserable when we signed the papers.
        (pauses)
That night I thought he'd never come back.

ELLA
But he did.

DORA
Things accumulated. I didn't pay attention, I chose not to pay attention.

ELLA
Hey listen, the flat's over and done with and he lasted away from you for what, three days. I know it sounds like a cliché, but, fighting is inevitable for every couple, but you come out of it stronger.

DORA
It's not just the flat. There's something else. Francine knows.

ELLA
I can't ask her right now, can I?

DORA
Remember when I was made partner two years ago? I had so many new responsibilities and I wanted to do well and I... I got pregnant. It was such bad timing. Theo wanted us to keep it.

A beat as Ella takes this in.

ELLA
If it wasn't right, it wasn't right. You've still got time.

DORA
I'm three years older than Francine.

ELLA
Yes, but they really wanted a baby, both of them. At the end of the day it's your body and Theo just has to understand.

DORA
He told me that he never got over it. That not keeping it was as if I rejected him.

Dora's phone rings.

DORA
It's Marcus.

Ella takes the phone and answers.

ELLA
Marcus, it's Ella. Wakey-wakey eggs and bakey. Francine has been in labour since eight (...) Dora and I are at the hospital, the waiting area, we're not allowed in(...) Everything is fine (...) Yes, I'll call you as soon as we get an update(...) Yes, any update. Where have you been by the way, we've been calling you for hours (...) Oh, OK(...) Yes, we'll call you or you can call us(...) Marcus! Congratulations.
(hangs up)
His phone died because he hadn't plugged in the adapter properly. Hopeless.

DORA
Crucifixion. That's how I would have killed Theo.

Ella sits down next to Dora. Pause.

ELLA
Come on Francine...

                    DORA
        Push!

                    ELLA
        You think she's in a lot of pain?

                    DORA
        She's strong...

                    ELLA
        She's the kindest...

                    DORA/ELLA
        Most caring child...

                    ELLA
        I'm gonna love this baby so much.

                    DORA
        Our little prince.

Pause.

                    ELLA
        I lied, the film doesn't pay.

                    DORA
        You'll get a good one soon.

Pause.

                    ELLA
        'Lord, we know what we are, but know not what
        we may be.'

                    DORA
        Hamlet?

                    ELLA
        Five points to Dora.

Pause.

                    ELLA
        I'll love your baby, too.

                    DORA
        And I'll love yours.

                    ELLA
        I don't want one.

                    DORA
        Of course not.

End of scene.

SCENE 2

A bedroom in an old house somewhere in the Greek countryside with a double bed, a wooden wardrobe, and a chest of drawers.

Ella Sienna, about 8 years old, stands on the bed covered with a sheet that makes her look like a nun. Francine Sienna, about 12 years old, sits on the bed as the audience for this private performance.

          ELLA
    (waving her hands ceremoniously)
 Oi - hei - hoi
 Mei - con - cou
 Mmmmmm
 Ola- kala - kei
 Mei - con -cou
 Mmmmmm

Francine bursts into laughter. Dora Sienna, about 15, enters, looking upset.

          DORA
 You're so loud.

          FRANCINE
 Sorry.

Ella, undefeated, continues.

          ELLA
 Oi - hei -hoi

Dora pulls the sheet off Ella, who loses her balance and falls, hitting her head on the bedrest.

          ELLA
    (cries)
 Agh!

Francine takes her in her arms.

          FRANCINE
 It's OK, my love.

          DORA
 I'm sorry Ella, it was an accident.

          ELLA
    (in tears to Dora)
 You're mean and fat!

          FRANCINE
 Dora didn't do it on purpose. And she's right.
 We were being loud. How would Mum feel if she
 heard us laughing?

DORA
She'd think you were making fun of Granddad.

ELLA
I was a priest doing a funeral, I was being serious!

FRANCINE
That's not how it seemed from the outside.

DORA
From the outside it seemed that you were being inconsiderate.

Ella calms down a little.

ELLA
I only wanted to understand...

FRANCINE
What did you want to understand?

ELLA
Nothing.

A knowing look between the elder sisters.

DORA
Did you want to play the priest so you could understand what happened earlier in the church?

ELLA
Yes.

Pause.

DORA
He was praying. In this culture, when somebody dies, priests pray for them.

ELLA
Was he talking to Granddad?

DORA
No.

ELLA
Who was he talking to?

FRANCINE
Who were you talking to when you were being a priest?

ELLA
(somewhat confused)
To you?

FRANCINE
Exactly. The prayers and the service in the church are for the living. To console them. To comfort them.

DORA
So now Mum feels better after Granddad's death. And we'll talk about him so that he stays alive in our memory.

Pause.

ELLA
I'll talk to him.

DORA
How will you do that?

Ella doesn't reply.

FRANCINE
You won't tell us your secret?

ELLA
I'll talk to him.

The three girls tuck under the covers. Pause.

ELLA
I'll talk to him in my secret language.

DORA
(whispers)
Kar - por - ter

FRANCINE
(whispers)
Pil - fil -kil

ELLA
(whispers)
Mmmmm
Hoi - hei mmmm

End of scene.

TAYLOR BEIDLER

Taylor Beidler is a playwright, performer, deviser and dramaturge hailing from New York City. Her work has been produced across the US and UK, and garnered recognition from the Kennedy Center American College Theatre Festival. She will be an artist-in-residence at BarnArts this summer. For more information, please visit www.taylorbeidler.com.

COKE BURNS BRIGHTEST ON THE ALLEGHENY

INT. THE DEN — AFTERNOON

A close-up from under the clear glass coffee table. A line of white powder is poured on top. Someone cuts it into a line, rolls a dollar bill. Close-up of a nose snorting a line, hairs and all. A finger grabs the rest.

> VERA (OS)
> Jesus, Jimmy.

CUT TO:

INT. THE DEN — SAME

Top-down view of the coffee table. SONNY (2) is sitting underneath, sucking his thumb. He's wearing a mini tuxedo. He's watched the whole thing.

JIMMY (31) is picking coke off his moustache. He sees Sonny.

> JIMMY
> Aw, hell, he don' know, baby.

VERA (27) walks down, picks Sonny up. She's in a pencil skirt and a cone bra. Sonny tries to adjust his body around her heavily wired tits. She's biting down on a Pall Mall.

> VERA
> You save some for me, sugar?
> (to Sonny)
> Did your daddy save any for me?

Jimmy takes the Pall Mall out of her mouth, sticks two powdered fingers in her mouth. He lets them linger. He turns the fingers in her mouth, makes his fingers look like
a gun, shoots in her mouth.

> JIMMY
> I love you.
> You shouldn't smoke in front of the kid.

He ties his tie, he wears a three-piece suit.

> VERA
> Janet say there's kiddy care?

                              JIMMY
                    Janet says a lot of things.

                              VERA
                    Don't start with me.

She puts Sonny down on a couch. The sofa cushions heave dust in their faces.
Leftover ash.

                              JIMMY
                    Baby, I gotta make a run.

                              VERA
                    Late already.

                              JIMMY
                    It's a very important order.

                              VERA
                    It's Maureen's wedding day.

                              JIMMY
                    We'll get there in time to see if this guy
                    makes it to the altar.

                              VERA
                         (between drags of a new cigarette)
                    'Least he proposed.

                              JIMMY
                    What's that?

Close-up of Sonny on the couch. He curls his hair and sucks his thumb. The voices of
Jimmy and Vera escalate but the words are incomprehensible. We hear a smack,
and something falling off the shelves.

                                                            CUT TO:

INT./EXT. FORD GRANADA — LATER

Sonny's in the middle seat. He's propped up with *The Joys of Cooking* cookbook.
Vera and Jimmy are in the front seat. Vera's lip is puffy. She's trying to cover
it up with lipliner in the overhead mirror. Jimmy is driving. The Doobie Brothers
plays on the radio.

                              JIMMY (CONT'D)
                    Five minutes.

He pulls over.

                              VERA
                    Gimme da keys.

                              JIMMY
                    No way.

                              VERA
              It's like 50 degrees out, Sonny will get cold,
              won't you Sonny?

Close-up of Sonny. He is playing with a toy truck. He nods without looking up.

                              VERA (CONT'D)
              You want him to freeze his little fonz off?

Jimmy hands over the keys.

                              JIMMY
              Don't waste non ennat gas, OK?

He pops a kiss on her.

                              JIMMY (CONT'D)
                      (to Sonny)
              You're man of the house while I'm gone.

EXT. A TWO-STOREY HOUSE — SIMULTANEOUS

A large man, clearly a bodyguard, walks out and waits on the porch. Jimmy walks out of the car. He jogs up the steps to the porch, they shake hands. The bodyguard pats him down. They go inside.

                                                          BACK TO:

INT./EXT. FORD GRANADA — SOME TIME LATER

Vera is almost through a Pall Mall, windows closed.

                              SONNY
              Mommy, I need to pee.

                              VERA
              Oh Christ, just hold it in, baby.

                                                          CUT TO:

Later. Vera is through several cigarettes, as indicated by the filled-up ashtray.

                              SONNY
              Mommy, I—

                              VERA
              I know, baby, I know.

                              SONNY
              I didn't make it.

                              VERA
              Oh, oh shit. It's OK baby, we'll get you
              cleaned up.

She looks out at the house. No sign of Jimmy coming out anytime soon.

Vera climbs over to the driver's seat.

                    VERA (CONT'D)
     Your daddy's an asshat, you know that?

EXT. THE MON RIVER — LATER

Sun setting on the steel mills off the Mon River, PA. Blue flames burn from the factories. A puff of steam from the burning slag.

We see the Ford Granada speeding down the interstate, cutting off other cars.

EXT. ST MARY IGNATIUS CATHEDRAL — LATER

The Ford Granada pulls into a parking spot with a hard stop.

Vera runs out, holding Sonny out in front of her so as not to get piss on her silk blouse.

INT. ST MARY IGNATIUS CATHEDRAL — MOMENTS LATER

Vera runs into the cathedral. The cathedral is now empty save the volunteers resetting the altar.

                    VERA (CONT'D)
     Fuck!

The volunteers stop and look at her.

                    VERA (CONT'D)
     Sorry.

She runs out, Sonny still outstretched.

EXT. CARRICK TOWNSHIP BINGO HALL — LATER

A changeable letter sign says 'congrtutions to the hppy cple.'

A signpost that reads 'Save Our Jobs!' is hammered into the charred grass outside.

The Ford speeds into a tight parking spot, scraping the neighbouring car.

Vera runs out, goes to pick up Sonny, lifting him on top of the car so she can sneak out of the tight spot. She picks him up again once she is around the other side.

INT. CARRICK TOWNSHIP BINGO HALL — MOMENTS LATER

A low-budget wedding reception. A sheetcake from Giant Eagle. An Iron City Beer keg. A disco ball rotates. A table is devoted to six-foot hoagies. There's a hard rock cover band.

MAUREEN (25), the bride, is wearing a wedding dress with extra tulle and a slit up the side. She's eating with her new husband, a slicked back receding hairline and sideburns.

Vera runs in with Sonny.

Maureen sees her. She glares at her, gives her a 'fuck you' gesture. She turns around and kisses her new husband.

JANET (28), Vera's friend, comes up to her. She's had a couple.

                    JANET
So glad you could join us.
        (to Sonny)
Come mere, baby.

                    VERA
Don't hug him, he pissed his pants.

                    JANET
Ah Jesus.
Where's the jagoff?

                    VERA
Take a wild guess.

                    JANET
Grab some cake, or whateva.
I'll clean the kid.
You better go talk to Daddy.

                    VERA
What's he need?

                    JANET
He's got some beef with you. He ain't too happy.

                                                    CUT TO:

INT. CARRICK TOWNSHIP BINGO HALL DANCE FLOOR — MOMENTS LATER

A close-up shot of an older man, MICK (72), wearing several class rings. He sits at the head of any table he goes to, including this one.

He's twirling the flower girl around his chair while smoking a stoagie. He's got an oxygen tank under the table.

                    VERA
Hey, Daddy.

                    MICK
        (slow to speak)
You my girl?

                    VERA
          Whaddya mean, Daddy?

Goes to kiss his cheek, he pushes her away.

                    MICK
          You my girl, right?

                    VERA
          What're you... Daddy, whaddya talkin' about?

                    MICK
          Come mere.

Pulls her closer to him, whispers.

INT. WOMEN'S BATHROOM — LATER

Janet has Sonny on the pull-down diaper changer.

                    JANET
          Jesus, you did a number, kiddo.

She tries to dampen his pants.

                    JANET (CONT'D)
          You talkin' yet?

Sonny doesn't know whether to reply.

                    JANET (CONT'D)
          Good. Quiet is good summa the time.
          Learn that already, eh?
          Your daddy can be a mean awful man sometimes.
          You know any ennat?

Sonny sits upright.

                    SONNY
          Daddy had party for me.

                    JANET
          What kinda party, baby?

                    SONNY
          He had lots of friends over.

Vera rushes in. She grabs Sonny.

                    VERA
          What kinda family is this, huh?

                    JANET
          Hey, hey—

Gestures to Sonny. Vera doesn't give a damn.

> VERA
> Y'all a bunch of snitches. Rattin' us out?

> JANET
> Shoulda thought about that before you shortchanged us.

> VERA
> Jimmy owns your ass, you know. He's the only one keeping food on our plates.

> JANET
> Cuz he couldn't keep a mill job if he tried. And believe me he tried.

Vera grabs Sonny from Janet. Vera spits in Janet's face.

> VERA
> We're stayin' afloat, is what we're doin'. And you? You sonsa bitches are just blood in the water, just wait. You'll be on your fucking knees.

INT./EXT./ FORD GRANADA — EVENING

Vera is driving back, this time with Sonny in the front seat, same propped-up cookbook. She is chainsmoking and speeding. She's makes a hairpin turn and holds Sonny upright with one hand.

EXT. TWO-STOREY HOUSE — LATER

Vera pulls up to the same house she dropped Jimmy off at. The lights are off. Vera drives away.

INT. THE DEN — LATER

Vera is waiting for Jimmy. She's smoking on the couch, no ashtray in sight. Sonny is under the table.

Sonny's POV. We see the door open. Jimmy walks in, a car speeds off in the distance. Jimmy has a black eye.

> VERA (OS)
> What the hell happened?

> JIMMY
> Just. Shut up, will you? Where's the kid?

> VERA (OS)
> He's in his room.
> What's this I hear about you holdin' money back from my sister, huh?

> Nunna them have jobs, Jimmy, they're tailin'
> us. They're just dumb enough to turn us in.

JIMMY
I don' need this right now, where's the baby?

VERA (OS)
He's sleepin'. I puttim, I puttim to bed
or somethin'.

JIMMY
Go check onnim. Go check onnim and lock
the doors.

VERA (OS)
Jesus, Jimmy, what's goin' on, heh?

JIMMY
Grab the kid, we're movin'.

VERA (OS)
I'm fuckin' done, you knowat?
Fuckin' done.

Camera follows her feet towards the hallway.

The camera is now also partially obstructed by a blanket, Sonny's POV looking up from underneath the glass table.

A long line of powder is poured and cut on the table. Same nose taking the same hit. A moment. Blood drips from the nose onto the table. Jimmy's face comes crashing onto the table. He's unconscious. The table cracks.

VERA (OS)
He's not in here!

Footsteps down the hall.

Vera screams off camera.

MAGDALENE BIRD

Magdalene Bird is a scriptwriter, activist and performer, devoted to the Arts and helping others. She co-created the XRT Festival and currently is a writer-in-residence with FLY Festival. She recently performed her writing at The Pleasance Theatre and is writing short films for Drama Studio London.

BABY BLUE
(a radio play)

SCENE 1: LIVING ROOM

> **FX: A CHILDREN'S TELEVISION SHOW PLAYS QUIETLY IN THE BACKGROUND.**
>
> **BABY'S BREATHING, QUICK AND A LITTLE RASPY.**

Stanley: Hey, beautiful, hello.
Where's Mummy gone? Is she in the bathroom?
The bathroooom?

> **FX: BLOWS RASPBERRIES.**
>
> **TABITHA ATTEMPTS TO REPEAT BUT WITH MORE SALIVA AND A SLIGHT HUM.**
>
> **FOOTSTEPS APPROACH.**

Anna?
Anna, love, what, what have you done?

Anna: I didn't like it.

Stanley: So you shaved it all off?

Anna: Don't pick her up.

Stanley: OK.

Anna: Please.

Stanley: I won't, love. Look, I'm stepping away.

Anna: She's been obsessed with the curtains today.

Stanley: Ah, maybe she'll become a designer — or something.
(*Pause*)
So where did you put it all?
(*Pause*)
The hair?

Anna: In the bin.

Stanley: Anna, this isn't...
I thought you were getting better?
How are you today?

Anna: You're home early.

Stanley: Love?

Anna: I'm sorry, I just...
(*Pause*)

Stanley: It'll get better.

Anna: I don't know anymore, Stanley.
I don't know anything.

SCENE 2: INT. THERAPIST'S OFFICE

FX: TABITHA'S BREATHING IS NOW HEARD THROUGH A MONITOR, IT IS MORE CRACKLED THAN BEFORE, IT SOFTENS AS OTHER NOISES JOIN THE ROOM.

A LOUD CLOCK TICKING.

WATER BEING POURED.

Dawn: Anna?

Anna: Yes?

Dawn: Would you like me to repeat the question?

Anna: No.

FX: TABITHA'S BREATHING BECOMES LOUDER, WE HEAR TABITHA BEGINNING TO STIR.

Dawn: Would you like to answer?

Anna: (*Pause*) No.

Dawn: Anna, the monitor is here for your support, not for protection.
(*Pause*)
Please.

FX: THE MONITOR BECOMES QUIETER AGAIN. WE HEAR SOMETHING THUD ONTO THE TABLE. A THROAT IS CLEARED.

Dawn: Anna, feelings are complicated.

FX: WATER IS GULPED. THE GLASS IS PLACED ON THE TABLE.

Anna:	Mhm.
Dawn:	(*prompting Anna*) And sometimes words don't do them justice.
Anna:	No. They don't.
Dawn:	But I can't help you if you don't talk. I'm not here to judge you. (*Anna scoffs*) I'm here to listen.
Anna:	You're here to judge and give advice or referrals or — something.
Dawn:	That's true, but I'm not against you, Anna. I'm here to help you, to help you reconnect to yourself and—
Anna:	It's just hair.
Dawn:	Yes it is, but I thought these sessions were going well, didn't you?
Anna:	I just, I, I just need sleep.
Dawn:	And why can't you sleep at the moment?
Anna:	I don't have enough time.
Dawn:	Anna, she's already five months old.
Anna:	Do you have children?
Dawn:	(*Pause*) No.

FX: A PEN IS CLICKED ON AND OFF.

Dawn:	(*clears her throat*) Anna, the focus needs to be on you.
Anna:	How do you know? You don't [have children. How do you—]
Dawn:	This form of aggression will not help you.

FX: MORE WATER IS POURED.

Anna:	Sorry.
Dawn:	That's fine. (*Pause*)
Anna:	I'm still not touching anyone. I can't.

Dawn: Do you want to?

Anna: No.

Dawn: You know this is a very common sign of—

Anna: I know.

Dawn: And this past week, have you been able to—

Anna: No.
(*Pause*)

Dawn: OK, well let's return to what we did last week. I want you to close your eyes.

Anna: OK.

Dawn: And imagine you are in a safe place. You are there, Tabitha is in your arms and there is Stanley. Remember this room is safe.
Now I invite you to focus on the temperature of the room,
the floor beneath your feet,
[the weight of Tabitha in your arms]

FX: OVER THE MONITOR WE HEAR TABITHA'S CRIES.

EVA: (*CROONING*) TABITHA, TABITHA.

Dawn: No Anna, Eva is there. You need to focus.

FX: THE CRIES TURN TO HAPPY GURGLING AND CLAPPING.

Dawn: Anna, don't, please stay here until our session is up,

Anna: She's crying.

Dawn: She was. Now close your eyes again and—

Anna: I can't.

Dawn: Please don't end another session... [short]

Anna: She needs me.

Dawn: You also need yourself, Anna.

Anna: I'm sorry, I've just—

FX: A DOOR CLAPS CLOSED.

SCENE 3: INT. CAR — LATER ON

>FX: WINDSCREEN WIPERS. THE HUM OF THE CAR. BREATHING. TABITHA'S QUICK BREATHS ARE QUIET IN THE BACKGROUND.

Eva: You remember my green hat?
The bobble one?
You can borrow it if you want?

Anna: I don't want to cover it.

Eva: No, I know, just for when it gets cold.
It might snow next week.
Could be nice — a day off work.
The whole world collapses due to an inch of snow.
(*Pause*)
They're expensive you know.

Anna: Sorry?

Eva: Don't apologise to me, I'm not paying for them.
You should use them though. Stop cutting them short.

Anna: Yeah.

Eva: I'm not here to tell you off, I'm not your mum, Anna. Jesus, Indicate! Stupid learner!

>FX: BEEPS HORN. TABITHA STARTS TO STIR AND CRY.

All I'm saying is there's no point in me taking time off to be there with Tabitha outside, if you're just gonna waste it. (in a soothing voice) Tabitha, hey Tabitha. You're OK.

Anna: She's fine.

>FX: A RATTLE IS HEARD.
>
>TABITHA QUIETENS BACK DOWN.
>
>THE TICK OF THE INDICATOR. HANDS MOVING ON LEATHER AS THE WHEEL IS TURNED.

Eva: Look, I'm only saying this because I care. If you just tried with the sessions, stayed for the whole hour—

Anna: Did Stan ask you to tell me off?

Eva: No he didn't, Anna.
(*Pause*) Look it's not healthy for Tabitha if you keep being like this. What happened, happened, it was sad, it was really sad and we wish you'd spoken to someone sooner, but it's over now, so you need to, you need to try. You need to actually try.

FX: THE HIGH-PITCHED GROAN OF THE CAR, THEN THE GEARS BEING CHANGED. THE SMOOTHER HUM AS THEY SPEED UP.

It's just not fair on Stanley.
(*Pause*)
Or Tabitha.
(*Pause*)
Anna?
(*Pause*)
Anna, I'd really like it if you responded. I know Stan puts up with this, but I'm trying to have an honest conversation with you.

FX: CLASSICAL MUSIC BEGINS TO PLAY OFF A PHONE.

Anna: It's healthy for Tabitha, apparently.

Eva: That's great, Anna, but could you reply?

Anna: There wasn't a question.

Eva: You know what I mean.
(*Pause*)

Anna: I'm fine. Thank you for driving us.

Eva: I don't need a thank you, I need to know if you're going to—

FX: THE VOLUME IS TURNED UP.

Anna: Oh, Tabitha loves this part.

Eva: Anna—

Anna: Don't you, sweetie. Look at that smile! God, that smile is heart-breaking.

SCENE 4: INT. COFFEE SHOP

> FX: CHINA CUPS CLATTERING AGAINST SAUCERS.
> SCATTERED CHATTER.
> COFFEE MACHINES HISSING AND GRINDING.
> QUIET, SMOOTH JAZZ FROM A RADIO.

Stanley: You're making this a lot more serious than it is. She's just tired.

Eva: So are you! You still turn up for work and—

Stanley: I need to—

Eva: All I'm saying is it's not the first few weeks anymore, Tabitha's five months old now.

Stanley: Nineteen wee—

Eva: —and Anna shouldn't be this, this non-existent person! She barely engages with anything, with anyone. And I know I'm not her favourite person but...

Stanley: [That's not true].

Eva: I mean, is she even talking to you?

Stanley: Yes, course she is. Pass me the sugar.

Eva: Stanley...

Stanley: I mean she's tired so we're not like we were before but I can normally help make her—

Eva: Stan, listen to yourself. You can't keep coaxing her; she's draining you emotionally, physically.

> FX: A TEASPOON CLINKS AGAINST CHINA.

Jesus Christ, she's draining me emotionally and I'm only with her occasion— [ally]

Stanley: You don't have to—

Eva: You've lost so much weight, Stan, you can't... can't do this on your own, and I want to help. Really I do, but I clearly have no impact on her, I just... She needs professional help.

Stanley: She has professional help!

Eva: It's not working.

Stanley: Jesus, she doesn't need a ward or anything. She's not going to try to—

Eva: —How do you know, Stan?

Stanley: She's better now, she's just tired.

Eva: Has she let you hold Tabitha yet?

Stanley: Yeah, of course.

Eva: Without her being in the room to watch?

Stanley: Yes, Eva, now let it go. We've just got a newborn, things are gonna be tough.

Eva: How long does she let you hold her?

Stanley: I don't count, you're being stupi—

Eva: For more than a few minutes?
(*Pause*)
She's not good for you.

Stanley: She's just having...

Eva: What if she'd gone through with it?

Stanley: Don't you dare, Eva, don't you bloody dare. She didn't and even if... Tabitha would've been fine. She's got me.

Eva: Fine. I won't get involved, I'll just play the part of taxi driver.

Stanley: Eva.

FX: ZIPPING OF A BAG.

Stanley: Eva.

Eva: Get a belt for those jeans.

Stanley: What?

Eva:	I can see your pants, Stan. Either gain weight or get a belt.
Stanley:	You sound like Mum.
Eva:	Mum would've been more demanding.
Stanley:	Sorry, Eva.
Eva:	It's fine.
Stanley:	Thank you for today.
Eva:	I didn't want... [you to]
Stanley:	I know. Get home safe.

FX: CHAIR SCRAPES THE FLOOR.

Eva:	No one would judge you if you left, Stan.
Stanley:	Don't...

SCENE 5: INT. KITCHEN – NIGHT

FX: THE SOUND OF VEGETABLES BEING CHOPPED AND SOMETHING SIZZLING.

EVERY TIME THESE NOISES QUIETEN, WE CAN HEAR THE NOISES FROM THE BABY MONITOR: BREATHING AND RUSTLING.

A FRONT DOOR IS HEARD OPENING AND CLOSING.

WE HEAR FOOTSTEPS (DRESS SHOES) APPROACHING.

Stanley:	(loudly) That bloody dog has taken a massive—

FX: CHOPPING STOPS.

Anna:	(loud whisper) Stan—
Stanley:	(quietly) Sorry, yes. Completely forgot. I mean I didn't forget, course that would be ridiculous, but the neighbours'... (pause) Sorry, did you have a good day?
Anna:	It was OK.
Stanley:	Did you get any sleep in the end?

Anna:	No.
Stanley:	Ah, OK.
Anna:	It's fine.
Stanley:	OK, well why don't you let me help with all this and you can have a nap? (*Pause*) Wow, this is a lot of garlic. Don't want to kiss me, eh? (*Pause*) Smells great though, love. (*Pause*) Do you want all the peppers done?

FX: CHOPPING RETURNS.

	Anna?
Anna:	Yes?

FX: CHOPPING STOPS.

Stanley:	Leave the monitor here, love. You need to sleep. I can—
Anna:	(loudly) Shh!

FX: TABITHA'S BREATH BECOMES LOUD, AS THE MONITOR IS BROUGHT CLOSER TO US.

	She just keeps stopping, she'll be breathing so fast and—
Stanley:	I know.
Anna:	It's crazy how fast she goes, like butterflies' wings or something, something more poetic than that, some word. I—
Stanley:	No, I know what you mean. It's beautiful but...
Anna:	But then it'll suddenly stop and...
Stanley:	Yes, but you...
Anna:	And then you suddenly think how fragile butterflies are.
Stanley:	Yes they are, but Tabitha's not actually—

Anna: And I don't want to wake her.

Stanley: Don't wake her.

Anna: But those seconds when she doesn't breathe is just...

Stanley: Terrifying, I know, but Anna she's not your metaphor, she's...

Anna: She just breathes so fast.

Stanley: That's normal though, she's absolutely fine, Eva said she—

Anna: She was round today.

Stanley: Did you not have a good time?

Anna: Yes, no, I mean no, I did have a good time. God, my brain is fucking useless at the moment. Just basic words are so, disappear, but yes it was fine.

Stanley: Fine?

Anna: A lot of words of wisdom.

Stanley: Ah, sorry...
Any of it actually... Oh bollocks, oh fuck, I've burnt the—
I'm sorry, love.
Love?

Anna: It's fine.

Stanley: I'm pretty sure we have more.

Anna: Maybe.

FX: FRIDGE DOOR OPENS, RUSTLE OF PLASTIC PACKAGING.

Stanley: Oh, we... Is this tea?

Anna: What?

Stanley: It was in the fridge.

Anna: (*exasperated*) Jesus.

Stanley: Don't [worry].

Anna: Don't what? I can't even make a goddamn cup of tea anymore.

Stanley: Hey, you never could make a good cuppa, too much [milk, too].

Anna: This isn't a fucking joke, Stanley!

Stanley: [Sorry, love].

Anna: I feel so fucking useless all the—
Don't apologise.

Stanley: Sorry.

Anna: No, I just mean... (*exasperated cry*) How am I meant to go back to work? I can't think straight, words, I can't even find basic bloody words, or shower, Stan, all I have to do is stand under the thing, and it's just... I can't, I can't do it, I can't do anything, I'm this useless ball of—

FX: TABITHA BEGINS TO STIR ON THE MONITOR.

Stanley: Anna, love, everything is OK.

Anna: No, it's not, Stanley, it's not. I'm not OK. I almost tried to...
(*pause*) I'm not.
I'm not me anymore.

FX: CRYING NOTICEABLE.

Stanley: Hey, love.
No, Anna, no stay here for a second.
Look, every new mum has this, this is normal.

Anna: [It's not normal, Stanley. Don't be such a, you're being a, I need to... Stanley]

END OF EXTRACT

ALICE COULTHARD

Alice Coulthard is an established actor and writer, currently studying a Scriptwriting Master's at UEA. In 2011, she played the title role in the national tour of *Keeler* and in 2016, she played the title role in *Finding Josephine*, winning the Grand Jury Prize at the Nashville Film Festival and Best Actress at Geena Davis's Women in Film Festival.

AFTERBIRTH

INT. HOSPITAL BIRTHING ROOM — NIGHT

A dimly lit birthing room, curtains closed. The sterile decor of an NHS hospital in need of updating. The unplaceable, uniform features of the institution lend an unnerving and surreal quality to the atmosphere. This could be anywhere in Britain.

A repetitive beep.

A hospital bed with a drip and an ultrasound machine attached.

Two midwives stand at the end of the bed with looks of composed anticipation on their faces.

A weary looking man, MARCUS (early 30s), stands at the side of the bed holding the hand of LLIANA (late 20s), who lies pale and pregnant, on her back. She stares at the foetal monitor.

She breathes with exhaustion. There is a sadness to her prettiness, weighed down by the pain in her face.

In the corner stands another woman, JUNE (60s), with a neat bob and pursed lips, looking nervous and wringing her hands. She is one of those women who always looks like she is about to dart forward and intervene, creating a constant sense of unease in any room she is in.

A beat and then the line on the foetal monitor begins to rise rapidly.

                    MIDWIFE 1
        OK darling, here it comes again. Annndd push!

Lliana pushes so hard she shakes and yells. Suddenly, a loud beeping sound from the heart monitor.

The midwives look at each other and one rushes out of the room.

MONTAGE. INT. HOSPITAL CORRIDORS/THEATRE ROOM — NIGHT. CONTINUOUS

Bright lights all around the hospital bed as it's rushed along a corridor. Several nurses and doctors run alongside, but their images are out of focus.

Then, another corridor, rushing past blurred patients and wards.

Then, under the bright, almost blinding lights of an operating theatre.

Then, at least ten nurses/doctors/anaesthetists rush around the bed as Lliana looks up at them, unable to move.

An anaesthetist administers a spinal block directly into her spine.

She is rolled onto a steel slab, stripped and her genital area shaved.

Noise and movement around her is distorted and out of focus.

INT. HOPSITAL WARD — NIGHT

The room has the dimly lit, surreal quality that we saw in the first scene. Sterile. Just a dull blue curtain separating this deeply private moment from the rest of the world.

A midwife holds a gurgling newborn baby at Lliana's breast. Lliana looks back and forth between the midwife and the baby with a stunned, blank expression.

Marcus is asleep, slumped in a chair next to the bed.

June stands on the other side of the bed watching closely and offering a hand to the baby's head a little more often than is necessary. Her timing feels awkward.

>   MIDWIFE 1
>   You just need to let the head come back
>   a little and then as his mouth opens...

The voice of the midwife fades into silence as she explains how to breastfeed, but her lips are still moving.

Lliana looks at her, blankly following instructions until suddenly she screams in pain.

Everything goes black.

FLASHBACK. INT. HOSPITAL ROOM — NIGHT

The room is dimly lit. Lliana is sitting beside the hospital bed this time, holding the hand of a woman, SOPHIE (late 50s), pale, eyes closed, shallow breathing.

Lliana's face is lighter here than we have seen so far, but the sadness creeps in at the corners of her mouth. She has placed a thick Aztec blanket over the sterile hospital sheets of her mother's bed. She smooths the edges. It gives a homely warmth to the room.

She takes some perfume out of her bag and gently dabs it on her mother's neck. She strokes her mother's forehead and kisses her cheek.

END FLASHBACK.

INT. HOSPITAL WARD — DAY

Lliana sits up in bed, pale and exhausted. June and Marcus sit next to her. June is holding the baby and feeding him with a bottle of milk, a look of intensity or determination on June's face.

                         LLIANA
I just don't understand why he won't...
I thought it would naturally...

Marcus strokes her hand.

                         MARCUS
It's going to be OK. We'll get there.

The midwife enters. She looks at June feeding the baby.

                         MIDWIFE 1
Oh. Lliana, have you managed to breastfeed
him yet? Formula really isn't the ideal...

June turns towards the midwife, almost blocking Lliana's view of their conversation. She speaks in hushed tones. Lliana can just make out June's words beyond her elbow which is in the way of their faces.

                         JUNE
The baby was screaming when I came onto the
ward. Lliana was fast asleep. She hasn't been
able to produce. Nothing. The main thing is
the baby doesn't starve, surely?

                         MIDWIFE 1
Lliana, did you manage to get anything out
at all?

                         LLIANA
Um. I don't know. It hurt, and then...
he wouldn't...

Marcus steps towards June.

                         MARCUS
Mum —

                         JUNE
We can try again in a bit. Let's just make
sure he's fed for now, shall we?

                         MIDWIFE 1
Do you want to try again now you've had some
sleep, Lliana? It really is best for his
immune system... for both of you.

June keeps feeding the baby with the bottle.

                    MIDWIFE 1 (CONT'D)
          Lliana?

                    LLIANA
              (Hesitantly)
          Yes. OK...

Lliana tries to sit up, but yelps in pain, clutching at her stomach.

The midwife takes the baby from June and passes him to Lliana. Lliana just stares at him.

                    MIDWIFE 1
          OK, darling. Remember what we said last night?
          Gently tilt the head back and let him
          come towards you...

A buzzing sound and then blackout.

FLASHBACK. INT. HOSPITAL ROOM — DAY

Lliana gently strokes Sophie's hand. Sophie looks faded and expressionless.

Lliana smiles gently.

                    LLIANA
          Mum. I've got some news.

Sophie turns her eyes to Lliana.

                    LLIANA (CONT'D)
          I'm pregnant.

Sophie's face falls. She looks away.

Lliana's smile fades. That wasn't the reaction she'd expected.

END FLASHBACK.

INT. HOSPITAL WARD — DAY

Lliana looks around her. June, Marcus and the midwife are staring at her. She looks down at the baby crying in her arms.

Her eyes are hot with tears of pain.

                    MARCUS
          Look I just don't know if this is going to
          work right now.

                    MIDWIFE 1
          If the baby doesn't get the colostrum in the
          first 24 hours it can be very damaging.

                              JUNE
                    (harsher tone)
                Let me take this from here, please. This is my
                daughter-in-law and my grandson, and I think
                if anyone is going to help her learn
                to feed her child...

The midwife looks at Lliana sobbing silently as the baby lies in her lap.

                              MIDWIFE 1
                OK, fine. But please try to get at least a
                little breast milk in that boy. It really is
                best for baby — and Mum.

The midwife leaves the room.

June watches her leave. She gently takes the baby from Lliana. Lliana stares at the baby with tears in her eyes but does not resist.

INT. MARCUS AND LLIANA'S FLAT, EAST LONDON — DAY

A darkened bedroom, curtains closed, but sunlight is streaming in through a crack between them.

Lliana wakes to the sound of June singing in the distance.

She sings 'Lavender's Blue, Dilly Dilly'.

She lies there for a moment, the sound becoming slightly distorted. She closes her eyes.

FLASHBACK. EXT. GARDEN — SUMMER'S DAY

A young Sophie sits on a swing under a tree with Lliana, aged four, on her lap.

Sophie is looking down into her eyes and singing the same lullaby we just heard.

The light is so bright we can barely make out their expressions but there is a sense of joy and serenity to the scene.

Suddenly a baby screams.

END FLASHBACK.

INT. LLIANA'S BEDROOM — DAY

Lliana tries to sit up with a jolt. She opens her eyes but the pain makes her yelp and clutch her stomach. She gasps for air, wide-eyed. She pauses awkwardly clutching her midriff and half-sitting on the bed.

She listens again.

We hear the lullaby come streaming into the room again. She looks at the baby cot. It is empty.

She rolls herself onto her side and pushes herself onto the floor, unable to use her stomach muscles to push herself up.

She lands on the floor, clutching her stomach in agony and crawls to the bedroom window.

She opens the curtains and blinding white light hits her.

The light fades a little to reveal June wandering the sunny garden with the baby in her arms, singing the lullaby to him.

INT. LLIANA'S BEDROOM — NIGHT

Lliana is on the bed again, propped up with pillows. The room is dimly lit with just a small bedside lamp on. The patterned soft furnishings and blankets make the room feel cluttered and claustrophobic rather than homely.

Marcus enters with a plate of food.

                    MARCUS
Here. You have to eat something.

                    LLIANA
Where is he now?

                    MARCUS
It's fine, he's with Mum. He's had another bottle, so he should sleep now.

Marcus smiles.

                    MARCUS (CONT'D)
He giggled earlier... honestly, I swear his little face was smiling.

Lliana's eyes fill with tears.

                    MARCUS (CONT'D)
It's OK... don't cry. He's fine.

                    LLIANA
But I haven't even seen him all day, your mum's just — I don't know... I need to try and feed him.

                    MARCUS
But you weren't producing any milk Li'. It's obviously not ideal but at least Mum's here to help out. You've been through a lot. You need to rest.

                    LLIANA
Can I see him?

                              MARCUS
                    Of course you can. Just try and
                    eat some of this pasta first...

He strokes her face.

                              MARCUS (CONT'D)
                    Look at me. He's wonderful. It's all gonna be
                    OK. Yeah?

Lliana looks unconvinced.

He helps her sit up a little, puts the tray with a plate of food on her lap and kisses her forehead.

He leaves the room.

She looks at the food a moment and pushes the tray aside. She sits and clenches her jaw in frustration.

She uses all her strength to push herself up and manages to walk, doubled-over to the bedroom door and opens it.

INT. MARCUS AND LLIANA'S FLAT, HALLWAY — NIGHT

Lliana shuffles out of the bedroom door, grimacing in pain, and holds onto the handrail at the top of the stairs.

She can hear the baby's gurgles from the downstairs living room.

She looks down, figuring out how to manoeuvre herself in her descent towards the living room.

She looks up and gasps in shock as she sees June standing right behind her.

                              JUNE
                    Do you need a hand?

The surprise makes Lliana's hand on the rail slip and she stumbles slightly.

June moves towards her as if to say something.

Buzzing sound over June's moving lips.

Lliana looks down the stairs and her vision sways with vertigo.

Blackout.

INT. MARCUS AND LLIANA'S FLAT, LIVING ROOM — NIGHT

Lliana opens her eyes to a DOCTOR (40s) holding a stethoscope on her chest. She looks down. Her breast is leaking milk onto her nightgown.

LLIANA

Where is he? I've got milk! I've — it's —
I can try and feed him!

She looks around her. The doctor and Marcus look at each other. The baby and June are nowhere to be seen. Lliana is wide-eyed with fear.

DOCTOR

Hello Lliana. Try to calm your breath a
little, we need to get your heart rate down.
You're OK, but you fell quite a way down those
stairs and you've reopened a part of your
C-section wound. You're bleeding again. It's
only a tiny bit but if your heart rate goes
up you will lose more blood.

LLIANA

Where's my baby?

Marcus and the doctor look at each other again.

MARCUS

Mum's taken him off for a bit. There's an
ambulance coming for you. We think it's best
you don't have to deal with Albie right now.

LLIANA

Albie?

MARCUS

Oh, sorry, that's just what Mum's been
calling him. When you get back from the
hospital we can talk properly about names.
I think it's quite cute though, don't you?

Lliana looks confused and scared. She shuts her eyes.

FLASHBACK. INT. HOSPITAL ROOM — NIGHT

The room is dimly lit. Sophie still has her head turned away from Lliana. Lliana's eyes are filled with tears.

END FLASHBACK.

EXT. OUTSIDE MARCUS AND LLIANA'S FLAT, EAST LONDON — NIGHT

A blue light flashes, lighting the whole street. Lliana is wheeled out on an ambulance stretcher. The baby's screaming cry continues. Lliana looks towards the sound and sees June pushing the baby in a pram back into the house.

LLIANA

I want to see him! Please!

                              MARCUS
                    As soon as they've sorted
                    you at the hospital. Don't worry, darling.
                    We'll be looking after him.

Ambulance doors slam shut.

THE END.

JACK MARCUS FITCH

Jack Marcus Fitch is an emerging writer for both stage and screen. He currently has two short films in production with Drama Studio London, *The Morning After the Night Before* and *Golden Gloves*.

A LIFE IN THE WEST

FADE IN:

EXT. FIELDS. MADDOX FARM. TEXAS — 1866 — DAY

A small, still puddle of dark water lay under the shade of long frontier grass.

Floating across the water's surface is a red ladybug, its legs kicking as it struggles.

Watching on is FRANCES MADDOX (6), a girlish picture of innocence with pale blonde hair.

With her index finger, Frances scoops the ladybug from the water and moves it carefully into the long grass.

                    ROBERT (OS)
    Frances!

EXT. CHICKEN COOP. MADDOX FARM — DAY

Running freely in a small wire enclosure attached to a wooden coop are three HENS and a COCKEREL, pecking at feed scattered across the floor.

The coop itself is attached to the back of a small farmhouse set amongst the surrounding fields. Two HORSES are tied up to a hitching rail at the side of the house.

Frances approaches the coop.

Her father ROBERT MADDOX (40s), a rugged man of the west wearing a STETSON HAT, tosses handfuls of wheat grain down to the chickens.

SUPERIMPOSE: 1866

                    ROBERT
    Here you are, and where did you get off to?

                    FRANCES
    There was a bug, I helped it.

                    ROBERT
          I thought you wanted to help me today?

                    FRANCES
          I do.

                    ROBERT
          Well that's good cause I've got something
          real important for you to do, OK?

                    FRANCES
          OK.

Lifting the lid on the coop, Robert reveals three nests each safely holding a number of eggs.

                    ROBERT
          Go on, carefully.

Placing her hand into the coop, Frances gently lifts the eggs from their nests, her face brimming with nervous excitement.

                    ROBERT (CONT'D)
          In here. Place them slow.

Robert gestures to a woven basket he's taken from beside the coop. Frances tenderly lays the eggs into the basket, concentrating, and careful not to crack them.

                    ROBERT (CONT'D)
          Good job.

Having taken all the eggs from the coop, Robert shuts the lid.

INT. KITCHEN. MADDOX FARMHOUSE — DAY

A ceramic plate topped with an omelette is slid in front of Frances, who sits waiting at a wooden table. Robert sits opposite with his own plate.

The kitchen surrounding them is a small, wooden-walled, homely environment.

Robert begins eating. Frances does not, preoccupied with a thought.

                    ROBERT
          Eat your food.

                    FRANCES
          Will you teach me how to ride soon?

                    ROBERT
          Not if you don't eat your food I won't.

Picking up her knife and fork, Frances quickly shoves in a forkful of food.

                    FRANCES
          Will you, please?

                              ROBERT
          One day, sure.

                              FRANCES
          No, soon, will you teach me soon?

                              ROBERT
          I'll think about it, all right?

                              FRANCES
          OK.

Beat.

                              FRANCES (CONT'D)
          Do you need any more help today?

                              ROBERT
          No that's OK, finish your food and go play.

Frances grins and eats her food.

EXT. FIELDS. MADDOX FARM — DAY

Frances runs and skips through the fields surrounding the farmhouse. She wears her father's Stetson hat, which sits too big on her head.

In her hand, she holds a toy, carved from a wooden block; it vaguely resembles the shape of a gun.

Periodically pulling the wooden gun from her hip, Frances pretends to draw it from an imaginary holster as she mimes firing shots off into the field.

                              FRANCES
          Bang, bang!

Hearing the sound of boots on the ground, Frances spins to see a man, WW (28), with dark hair and dressed in leather. Low on his neck he bears the mark of a brand, TWO OVERLAPPING Ws.

A COLT ARMY MODEL 1860 PISTOL hangs from his hip.

Drawing her toy gun from its imaginary holster once more, Frances points it at the man.

                              FRANCES (CONT'D)
          Put 'em up!

                              WW
          Don't shoot!

WW stops in his tracks. Playing along, he puts his hands up.

Looking behind WW, Frances notices four more men standing some way behind, each bearing a branded mark of their own OVERLAPPING INITIALS: CM / KS / PJ / NW.

                    WW (CONT'D)
          I like your gun. Did you make that yourself?

Frances stares back at WW, unsure what to make of him.

                    WW (CONT'D)
          Do you wanna see mine?

Slowly drawing the Colt Pistol from its holster, WW crouches, inviting Frances forward to take a look.

                    WW (CONT'D)
          Come on, here. You ever held a real
          one before?

Placing the weapon in her small hands, WW allows Frances to inspect the gun.

                    FRANCES
          No, my dad says it's too dangerous and that
          I'm not old enough.

Assisting Frances, WW cracks the top of the barrel away from the handle exposing six .44 calibre rounds loaded into a cylinder chamber.

                    WW
          Your daddy sounds like a smart man.

Taking the gun back into his own hands, WW spins the cylinder and flicks it back into place before depositing it back into its holster.

Emerging from the farmhouse, Robert approaches; a COLT 1851 NAVY REVOLVER hangs by his waist.

                    ROBERT
          Is there something I can help you
          gentlemen with?

As Frances begins to walk over to her father, she's grabbed by WW, who lightly pulls her back, holding her in front of him.

                    WW
          Is that your daddy?

Frances nods up at WW.

Robert stops some thirty feet away from WW, the makings of a stand-off.

                    ROBERT
          What can we do for y'all?

                    WW
          Well, that depends.

                    ROBERT
          On what?

                    WW
          Just you living here?

                    ROBERT
          Me and my little girl.

                    WW
          No wife?

                    ROBERT
          No.

                    WW
          You got any horses? Silver?

                    ROBERT
          No. Few chickens here is all, just enough for
          me and the girl to get by.

                    WW
          You ain't lying to me?

                    ROBERT
          No reason to.

Grabbing Frances under the chin, WW pulls up, forcing her to look at him eye to eye.

                    WW
          Your daddy ain't lying to me, is he?

Frightened and held tight, Frances struggles to shake her head 'no'.

                    WW (CONT'D)
          Good.

WW lets go of Frances and relaxes.

A moment of silence, broken by the neighing of horses on the other side of the farmhouse.

Robert's eyes meet WW's, whose face is a picture of disappointment.

                    WW (CONT'D)
          I hate liars.

Scrambling, Robert's hands fumble to draw the Navy Revolver from his waist. His hand finds the handle and he draws.

A bang ripples out across the fields as a hole is blown through the chest of the mid-draw Robert, his body sent spinning face-first into the dirt.

Standing opposed to the fallen body is WW, arm outstretched, clutching the Colt Pistol that previously hung from his hip. Frances is once again held back by his free hand.

Frances lets out a scream as she struggles to break free, desperate to get to her father.

                              WW (CONT'D)
          Sorry, little lady.

Holding Frances back, WW whips the butt of his pistol across the side of her temple, cracking her skull.

As Frances's body drops limp into the dirt CUT TO—

EXT. AMERICAN FRONTIER. TEXAS — DUSK

A panoramic view of the great stretching plains of the American Frontier spanning out across the horizon.

All we hear is wind rushing over grass.

A slow pan across the vista reveals a distant, isolated figure.

Stationary, a rider and his horse. The rider is ELI SHORE (25), wearing riding gear and a drifter hat.

Pinned to his chest is a silver US MARSHAL'S BADGE, catching the light of the setting sun.

Eli looks out over the frontier. A pillar of rising black smoke pours up from over the crest of the land and leaks into the sky.

Kicking his horse into action, Eli rides hard towards the climbing smoke.

EXT. FIELDS. MADDOX FARM — DUSK

Flakes of ash fall like snow over the fields of Maddox Farm.

Set ablaze, the farmhouse stands smouldering amongst the farmlands, spitting flame and smoke.

Riding at pace through the fields, Eli spots a body.

Robert Maddox lays flat, face up on the ground, eyes closed. Spotting the corpse, Eli rushes towards it and dismounts.

Investigating the body, Eli finds the spread of blood on cotton from a small bullet wound through Robert's chest.

Eli's attention is caught by small bloody handprints marking Robert's shirt.
He runs his fingers over the spots where the shirt was grasped.

Turning away from the body, Eli's face is met with a stunned look.

Facing him from across the farmland is Frances, ash faced and bloodied.
She cries silently as she stares at Eli who still stands over her father.

Eli rushes to Frances, crouching to her eyeline.

Frances embraces him in a panicked hug, crying into his shirt, her hands leaving small bloodied prints.

                              ELI
                    All right. It's all right.

EXT. AMERICAN FRONTIER. TEXAS — DUSK

Mounted atop Eli's horse, both he and Frances ride away from the burning
Maddox Farm.

Eli holds gentle control of the reins as Frances, sat side on, clings tightly
to Eli with tears on her face, blood dried to her face from the wound on her head.

The sun sets, dipping over the horizon.

EXT. RIO GRANDE CITY. TEXAS — NIGHT

Riding under dark skies, Eli takes the horse through the centre of Rio Grande
past housing, a bank, a brothel and the saloon of a hard-edged border town.

Drunks and whores line the streets, bottles in hand, laughing,
kissing and fighting.

Frances clings to Eli as they ride together, her eyes shut as she sleeps.

I/E. STABLES. RIO GRANDE CITY — NIGHT

A wooden stable stands at Rio Grande's edge, a series of stalls home to the
city's horses.

Riding slowly, Eli guides his horse into an empty stall filled with hay and
a water trough.

Dismounted, Eli carries Frances, still sleeping, over his shoulder as he closes the
gates to the stables.

INT. ELI's HOUSE. SPARE BEDROOM — NIGHT

Gently laying Frances down into a bed, Eli covers her small body with a sheet,
setting her to sleep.

He then moves to open a set of window shutters, allowing softly falling moonlight
to stream into the room.

Sitting on the bed's edge, Eli tenderly takes a damp cloth across the small
girl's temple, wiping the blood from her wounded face.

Leaving the room, Eli pulls the door closed on the peaceful Frances, sleeping
bathed in moonlight.

INT. ELI'S HOUSE. SPARE BEDROOM — 1882 — DAY

Moonlight dissipates, replaced by beams of sunlight glaring in through the
shutters, illuminating the room in a golden hue.

The interior of the bedroom is altered by the passage of time. The bed where Frances once slept is laid empty, the sheets roughly pulled back, disturbed.

EXT. OUTSKIRTS. RIO GRANDE CITY — DAY

A wide panorama of sand and dust and rock somewhere along the US-Mexico border.

Heat shimmers as it rises from the ground, distorting the line of the horizon.

Amidst the sparse expanse, an alignment of tin cans and glass bottles stand atop a run of half-destroyed, long-abandoned fencing.

A series of six quick-fire shots rips through the air, echoing out into the surroundings as four glass bottles explode from the fence posts they stand on.

One eye shut tight, the other eyeing the length of a REMINGTON MODEL 1875 REVOLVER's smoking barrel, a twenty-two-year-old woman, dirty blonde hair, a deep red scar across her temple.

It's Frances.

SUPERIMPOSE: 1882

Sixteen years have passed.

                       ELI (OS)
        You missed two.

Eli, now in his forties, stands behind, watching on with experienced eyes.
A US Marshal's badge is still pinned to his chest.

Pulling a second, twin Remington revolver holstered upon her waist, Frances fires off two more shots, nailing two more glass bottles.

                       FRANCES
        Good job I carry two guns.

                       ELI
        Good job the bottles don't shoot back.

                       FRANCES
        I got 'em, didn't I?

                       ELI
        You won't always get two tries.

Pulling back a corner of his collar, Eli reveals a scar left by a bullet marking the top of his chest.

                       FRANCES
        I know.

                       ELI
        You rushed. Take your time, breathe.

                              FRANCES
                    I know.

                                ELI
                    Again.

Holstering her spare weapon, Frances goes about removing the cylinder from her
revolver and reloads the cartridge.

NATALIE FROOME

Natalie Froome is passionate about television dramas that entertain, surprise, blur genres and reflect the modern world. Her scripts have been performed at RADA, The Pleasance London and Norwich Arts Centre. She was shortlisted for Channel 4's *4Stories* scheme in 2018 and she's recently been longlisted for Sid Gentle's *Thousand Films* contest. www.nataliefroome.com

INFLUENCE

EXT. LONDON. NIGHT.

Aerial shots of the London skyline, spectacular views of the financial heart of the City from the East End.

It's late, but lights blink out from every building.

INT. FLATSHARE — CORRIDOR. SHOREDITCH. NIGHT.

A house party rages in a hipster flat.

The central corridor is crammed with young people having a good time: making out, drinking, chatting animatedly. Music blares.

We track through the corridor, taking in the vibe.

Looking left and right, we see the KITCHEN, BATHROOM and BALCONY, all full of people.

Then we go through a closed door at the end of the corridor into...

INT. FLATSHARE — LIVING ROOM. CONTINUOUS.

...And the good-time atmosphere abruptly ends.

We're in a cosy, stylish living space: upcycled industrial coffee table, sofas.

Unlike the rest of the flat it's not crammed with people — just four young women: MO BARNES(23), RANI KOTECHA (23), BECCA MULLINS (25), and ZARA HARRINGTON-WELLS (24), in varying degrees of distress and shock.

They're looking down at someone (we can't clearly see who yet) lying motionless on the floor.

The low thump of music from the party creeps in.

A SPATTER OF BLOOD is on the corner of the coffee table.

The women look at each other. A few tense beats, shock wearing off to make way for dread.

Finally:

                        MO
      What do we do now?

No one has an answer.

                                            CUT TO BLACK.

EXT. BLOCK OF FLATS. SHOREDITCH. DAY.

BUZZZ! An intercom rings.

Cut wider to reveal a modern, mid-rise block in a side street. Mo stands at the main door with a backpack and suitcase.

SUPER: ONE WEEK EARLIER...

It clunks open and Becca is there. She's Mancunian, friendly.

                      BECCA
      Hi! You must be Mo.

                       MO
      Yeah, hi, Rebecca Mullins? We talked on Facebook.

Mo puts out a hand to shake.

                      BECCA
      Yep, but call me Becca, I'm Becca to everyone.

Becca pulls her into a hug.

                 BECCA (CONT'D)
      And I'm a hugger, not a shaker!

Mo's finding it awkward, but tries to be friendly. Becca lets go.

                       MO
      Right. Ha.

                      BECCA
      Come on then, after you.

Mo goes through the door, followed by Becca.

INT. FLATSHARE — CORRIDOR.

When it's not crammed with people, the corridor is just functional and every room leads off from here. Mo and Becca have just come through the door at one end.

                 BECCA (CONT'D)
      Just leave your stuff there, I'll introduce
      you to the others.

Mo leaves her suitcase and backpack by the door.

Becca opens the first door to reveal a bathroom.

                        BECCA (CONT'D)
    Bathroom's in there.

She moves on, knocks on the next door.

                        BECCA (CONT'D)
    And this...

                        ZARA (OS)
    Yeah?

Becca opens the door.

                        BECCA
    ... Is Zara.

Mo and Becca look through into ZARA'S BEDROOM — it's the biggest in the flat, and very stylish. On her plush double bed, a bunch of online clothes packages are piled up.

Zara herself stands in front of a giant mirror and a DSLR on a tripod. She's wearing a brand new outfit.

                        ZARA
    Can you actually wait for me to say to come
    in before—
        (then, spotting Mo and smiling)
    Oh, hi. You're the new housemate, right?

                        MO
    Yeah. Hi.

Zara shakes her hand.

                        ZARA
    Zara Harrington-Wells.

                        MO
    Nice to meet you. I'm Mo.

                        ZARA
    What's that short for?

                        MO
    Hm?

                        ZARA
    Well, you're not actually called Mo are you.

                        MO
    My full name is Morwenna Barnes.

                    ZARA
          Oh, Lord. Doubt you've forgiven your parents
          for that one.

Mo blinks.

A commotion further down the corridor grabs everyone's attention.

A door has just opened and a very angry half-dressed man bursts out, holding his T-shirt in his hand. This is LUKAS WEST (29, tattoos, hothead).

He heads towards the front door, yelling back.

                    LUKAS
          Delete me! Delete my contact!

He opens the front door to go, but wait, one more thing to say...

                    LUKAS (CONT'D)
          I never want to hear from you again.

And he slams it.

... Then realises his shirt is caught in the door. The handle clunks down as he tries to open the door from the outside.

A beat.

The doorbell rings.

Becca goes to the door and opens it a crack so Lukas can pull the shirt through.

                    LUKAS (OS) (CONT'D)
              (quietly)
          Thank you.

Lukas closes the door — without slamming it this time.

                    ZARA
          Wow...

In unison Zara, Mo and Becca look back towards where Lukas came from.

Rani stands in the doorway to her room, half-dressed too. She shrugs.

                    RANI
          He'll be back.

INT. FLATSHARE — LIVING ROOM. EVENING.

Zara and Mo sit in the living room, the ice has broken slightly. Zara is tapping away at a tablet, ordering a takeaway.

Becca enters and puts two mugs of tea down on the industrial coffee table we saw earlier.

                              MO

    Thanks.

Becca sits.

                            BECCA

    So, are you nervous? About tomorrow? New job,
    new people, all of that...

                              MO

    Well I mean, I've met all of you guys which
    is nice. Y'know, living together and working
    together.

                            BECCA

    Inspyred is like that, it's like a family.

                            ZARA
        (drily)
    A fuckin' weird family.

Becca laughs.

                            BECCA

    That's true. Anyway, I'm not in tomorrow.

                              MO

    You're part-time?

                            BECCA

    Zero-hours contract. But it lets me have time
    off for auditions.

                              MO

    Oh?

                            BECCA

    I'm an actor, well, trying to be anyway.

Zara holds the tablet up.

                            ZARA

    Who put a cheese naan? D'you want to share one?

                            BECCA

    That's me. Let's get one each, you can leave
    half for tomorrow.

                            ZARA

    It doesn't taste the same the next day though
    and I can't eat a whole one. That's like,
    a million calories.

                              MO

    I'll share one with you if you want?

                         ZARA
    Fab.

Becca yells out the door.

                         BECCA
    Rani, we're getting takeaway.

Rani enters, drying her hair with a towel.

                         RANI
    I've got food in the fridge.

She leaps onto the sofa, tucks her feet up, continues drying and combing her hair.

                         ZARA
              (clicking the tablet)
    In that case, food is on its way!

                         RANI
    You guys giving Mo the lowdown on work? The
    lucrative world of influencer management?

                         MO
    They are.

                         RANI
    Have they talked to you about Adam yet?

                         MO
    He's the boss, yeah? I met him at my interview.

                         RANI
    What did you think?

                         MO
    He's... a character.

                         ZARA
    That's one way of putting it.

                         MO
    He kept going on about the spelling,
    'inspired, with a y.'

                         ZARA
    He thinks it's edgy. You know, he doesn't
    like being called the CEO — I've heard him
    call himself 'The Captain'.

                         RANI
    That man is embarrassing.

Rani's phone bleeps.

She picks it up, laughs.

                        ZARA
            Lukas?

                        BECCA
            Definitely Lukas.

                        RANI
            Yep. Lukas.

                        MO
            Who's Lukas?

                        BECCA
            Y'know...
                (impersonating Lukas)
            'Delete me, delete my contact.'

They laugh.

INT. FLATSHARE — MO'S BEDROOM. DAY.

Beep be-beeeep! An alarm clock shrieks.

Mo emerges from the covers and slams the alarm off. The display reads 7:00.

EXT. BLOCK OF FLATS. SHOREDITCH. DAY.

The display of a phone: 7:01.

It's Rani's phone in her hand as she shuts the main door of the flat and heads towards a BIKE RACK.

As she unlocks her bike, a lady with a walking stick and a slobbery GREAT DANE on a leash approaches the flats. This is BARBARA (65).

                        RANI
            Morning!

                        BARBARA
            I heard your lot again last night, you need to
            keep the noise down.

                        RANI
            Very sorry about that Barbara. You have
            a good day.

As Rani walks her bike away, she taps on her phone, sending a message to FLAT GROUP CHAT which flies up as text on screen: 'Batty Barb is at it with noise complaints again.'

She puts earphones in and music starts as she cycles away (music continues over the next few scenes).

INT. FLATSHARE — BATHROOM. DAY.

Mo looks in the mirror above the sink.

She takes a deep breath like 'come on, you got this' and turns the tap on.

EXT. SHOREDITCH PARK. DAY.

A green space in the middle of the city. Joggers and commuters pass through.

Rani cycles through the park. She goes fast, relishing the morning air.

EXT. SHOREDITCH HIGH STREET STATION — PLATFORM. DAY.

Becca, takeout coffee in hand, waits for a train amongst a crowd of office types and creatives.

INT. FLATSHARE — ZARA'S ROOM. DAY.

Zara pops two green and white pills out of a packet labelled Fluoxetine and swigs them down with orange juice.

She picks up a slim laptop and shoves it in her bag.

EXT. REGENT'S CANAL — CITY ROAD BASIN. DAY.

The ex-industrial heartland of East London. Factories (most now converted into flats) back onto the canal.

Rani cycles along the towpath, passing a graffitied lock.

INT. TRAIN CARRIAGE. DAY.

Becca stands in the middle of a commuter crush on the overground train.

She silently mimes lines she's trying to remember.

EXT. BLOCK OF FLATS. SHOREDITCH. DAY.

Music fades as Zara and Mo leave the block.

Mo looks at her phone.

                    MO
        Maps says it's a 20-minute walk, is that
        about right?

                    ZARA
        Oh hun, it's your first day. I ordered an
        Uber. Come with.

                    MO
          (embarrassed)
     I just can't really afford to—

Zara waves a hand.

                    ZARA
     I've got it covered.

A car pulls up.

EXT. INSPYRED OFFICES. DAY.

The trendiest office building you could imagine. It's made out of four converted shipping containers set side by side, with glass panels on one end. The whole set-up is nestled between converted factories and overlooks the canal.

INT. INSPYRED OFFICES. DAY.

White walls, Mac computers and bright lights. A neon sign reading 'INSPYRED'. From the inside, you can't really tell you're inside shipping containers. Everything about this open-plan office screams young internet start-up company.

Beyond an obscured glass partition is the office of ADAM SUTCLIFFE (35), the CEO.

Adam's at his desk, feet on the table, making a phone call.

                    ADAM
          (into phone)
     I'm sure there's nothing to worry about.
     These things blow up quickly online, but they
     also blow over quickly. Honestly, give it a
     day or so and it'll be forgotten about.

We hear someone else come into the main offices, so does Adam.

                    ADAM (CONT'D)
          (into phone)
     I can hear our client manager coming in now.
     I'll send her to pick Craig up and we'll take
     things from there.
          (he listens)
     No, just... I don't want you to do anything
     you regret. I understand your position, but
     let's not be hasty.
          (pause)
     OK. OK, sure. Thank you. See you later.
     Bye then.

Adam cuts the call and leaps up, sticks his head out into the main office area.

                    ADAM (CONT'D)
     Rani!

Rani appears from a door with a shower/toilet symbol on it.

                    ADAM (CONT'D)
          I need you to go to Bethnal Green police station
          and pick up Craig Owens.

                    RANI
          What?

                    ADAM
          He's been arrested and his sponsors are
          kicking off.

                    RANI
          I'll just have a quick shower, cycled five
          miles this morning—

                    ADAM
          No, now. Forget the shower, go.

                    RANI
          But—

                    ADAM
          Redstone Clothing are threatening to pull
          their entire investment in him. There's a lot
          of capital at stake here.

                    RANI
          All right. All right.

                    ADAM
          Not trying to be the bad guy, I'm just trying
          to keep this ship afloat, Rani.

                    RANI
          Give me two minutes.

Rani goes to her desk, grabs a can of deodorant from her desk drawer and sprays it up her top, then starts packing things from her desk in her bag.

Zara and Mo enter the office. Zara has a Starbucks in hand.

                    ZARA
          Hey, hey, hey, it's a brand new day!

She senses the tense mood.

                    ZARA (CONT'D)
          What?

                    ADAM
          Zara, I need you on the phones immediately.
          Any calls about Craig Owens, you sweet talk
          them, OK? Use all the PR bullshit you can
          think of. We cannot lose control of this.

                    ZARA
          Craig Owens? The parkour guy?

                    RANI
          Yep, he got arrested.

                    ZARA
          For...?

                    ADAM
          Aggravated trespass. Police picked him up off
          a building site. Canary Wharf.

Rani has her bag, she heads out of the office.

                    ZARA
               (sarcastic)
          Perfect. Nothing like a crisis to kick off
          a Monday morning.

Adam calls after Rani.

                    ADAM
          Bring him back here straight away, and don't
          let him tweet anything.

Rani gives him a mock-salute, leaves.

Mo is just standing there awkwardly, not knowing what to do.

Adam notices her.

                    ADAM (CONT'D)
          Ah! Yes. I'm afraid you're getting thrown
          in the deep end today Morwenna.

                    MO
          It's Mo, please.

                    ADAM
          Welcome to Inspyred.

SAI HAVAL

Sai Haval is an award-winning director, writer and producer who likes to offer her audience a window to peep into Indian culture and sensibilities. She worked as a 'creative producer' for three years in a boutique film house and recently completed her MA in Scriptwriting from the University of East Anglia. Here are the links to her work: www.imdb.com – sai haval | www.vimeo.com/saihaval.

A MEMORY OF A CUPBOARD

NOTE: THE DIALOGUES IN THIS SCRIPT ARE SPOKEN IN HINDI AND SUBTITLED IN ENGLISH.

FADE IN:

INT. CLINIC — DUSK

A distorted gaze wanders around the room.

White walls and tiled floor. Medical degrees on the wall. A pen, pencil, timer and a notepad.

DR DIXIT, 40s, well dressed, clears his throat and the gaze settles on him.

> DR DIXIT
> I'm going to ask you a few questions like I did in our last session. These are just some memory exercises. It's OK if you don't remember the answers. Just relax. All right?

He clicks the timer, opens his notepad and turns a page.

INTERCUT — INT. KITCHEN/DINING ROOM, MOHAN'S HOUSE — DAY

He begins to write. His fingers tremble. Writes in a wobbly handwriting. Stops. Frowns.

Begins again but it's still shaky. He frowns more.

> INTERCUT

Bright sunlight glares through a window. Tea boils in a saucepan.

> INTERCUT

Mohan retraces a previously written word in a crossword, now flawlessly. Fluttering of wings followed by cooing of a pigeon is heard. He looks up.

> INTERCUT

A pigeon sits between the wooden bars of the window. A pair of woman's hands shoos it away. Then she pours the tea into three cups. Her gold bangles shine in the sunlight.

INTERCUT

Mohan looks up as his wife, MEERA, 65, approaches with teacups. She wears a simple sari and her white hair is tied in a tight bun. WIDE ANGLE of the room. A house with wooden doors and windows, old style. Stained glass windows give the house a warm yellow tone.

Mohan looks back at the puzzle and his eyes frantically look for empty blocks. He finally locates a blank word, and writes with shaky handwriting. Passes the newspaper to Meera.

                    MOHAN
          I completed it.

She faintly frowns, something bothers her but she ignores it.

                    MEERA
          This wasn't difficult at all!

ANIKA enters hurriedly, an attractive woman in her late 30s. Drops her bags on one chair and plonks herself on the other. Grabs a cup of tea, takes a biscuit from a container. Dips it in the tea and it falls inside.

                    ANIKA
          Shit!

Her phone buzzes. She reads the messages. Mohan peeks into her phone.

                    MOHAN
          Is that Sameer?

                    ANIKA
              (Calmly)
          Stop spying on me, Baba.

She takes out the mushy biscuit with a spoon, licks it.

                    MOHAN
          Who is it then?

Anika shoots him a look.

                    ANIKA
          The carpenter.

Anika serves herself porridge.

                    ANIKA
          He called me yesterday. And Maa, if you
          don't know, Baba wants to make a 'Victorian'
          looking cupboard for your bedroom.

                    MOHAN
          What's wrong in a Victorian cupboard?

                    ANIKA
          Nothing's wrong in a cupboard. You told him

                    you'll make it with him. Also, why do you need
                    one?

                              MEERA
                    Yes, why do we need one?

Meera and Anika stare at Mohan.

                              MOHAN
                    Aaa... well...

Meera and Anika exchange looks.

                              MOHAN
                    When I was young, our neighbour, aaa... his
                    name... his name... Yes! Mr Tadiwala. He had
                    a... beautiful cupboard. He always gave me
                    sweets from it. I want the same one.

Anika gets up, puts her plate on the kitchen counter.

                              ANIKA (OS)
                    Baba, if you want a vintage looking one,
                    there're shops which sell those. You don't
                    need to make one.

                              MOHAN
                    But I want to make one, what's your problem?

                              ANIKA
                    All right then. You don't want to listen
                    to anyone.

Anika gulps some water, gathers her stuff and slams the door behind her.

                                                          FADE TO BLACK

                              MOHAN
                    Why is she getting angry?

                              MEERA
                    Don't drag me in the middle. Finish your tea
                    and then go shower.

TITLE: A MEMORY OF A CUPBOARD

EXT. OLD MARKET — DAY

An over-crowded street, crammed with crumbling shops on either side.
Anika and Mohan make their way through the crowd.

They turn around a corner and enter a lane with antique shops. KISHAN is seen
waving at them, a skinny, curly-haired boy in his 30s.

                    KISHAN
          Namaste chachaji! How are you?

Anika smiles courteously, checks her watch.

                    ANIKA
          Kishan, let's get going quickly.
          I don't have much time.

Kishan obediently nods.

                    MOHAN
          I told you, I want to take my own
          time. You can go if you want.

                    KISHAN
          Chachaji, this way...

They get on the main road and merge in the crowd.

INT. ANTIQUE SHOP — DAY

A dark dingy shop, old and broken furniture scattered around. Mohan stands in front of a tall wooden cupboard. Kishan anxiously stares at him. Anika stands calmly in one corner, eating a bar of chocolate.

                    MOHAN
          Not this.

Mohan walks out. Kishan looks disappointed. Anika gestures at him to stay calm. They follow him out.

SHOP 2:

Mohan walks in. Anika and Kishan follow him. INSERT of a cupboard. Slightly more modern looking than the previous one. He begins to walk around it.

SHOP 3:

CONTINUOUS FROM PREVIOUS SHOT — Mohan completes his round around a different cupboard. Smaller than the rest but perfectly Victorian style.

                    MOHAN
          Kishan, none of these are good! Do you
          understand Victorian? Means from the time
          of British.

                    KISHAN
          But... all these are...

                    ANIKA
          Baba, why are you being difficult? At least
          tell him what's wrong.

                    MOHAN
          The first one had not so nice door.

                    And the second one was very modern. This
                    one is Victorian but too small. And I want
                    something taller and wider than this.

                              ANIKA
                    Baba, something bigger than this won't fit
                    through our door.

Mohan ignores her and carefully inspects the cupboard. He gently touches the wood.
His fingers tremble.

Suddenly, he stands still, staring at the cupboard vacantly. Disoriented.
Anika's distorted and faint voice.

                              ANIKA
                    Baba, let's move ahead.

Pause.

                              ANIKA
                    Baba...

Anika taps on his shoulder. Mohan gets back to normality.

                              MOHAN
                         (Mumbles)
                    ... I am thinking.

CLOSE ANGLE of his hand. He opens a drawer.

INT. BEDROOM, MOHAN'S HOUSE — DAY

CLOSE ANGLE of a drawer opening. Mohan shuffles the things inside. Shuts it.
He paces around the room, opening all the cupboards, shelves and drawers.

                              MOHAN
                    Meera!

No response.

                              MOHAN
                         (Agitated)
                    Meera!

Mohan sits on the floor and searches through the lowest compartment of a shelf.
Meera's shadow softens the light. Mohan looks up.

                              MOHAN
                         (Blankly)
                    Where is my phone? You were using it
                    yesterday.

                              MEERA
                    I must have given it back.

Mohan gets up, dusting the back of his pyjamas.

                    MOHAN
          (Sternly)
     No you didn't.

                    MEERA
     I'm sure I did.

He holds Meera gently by her shoulders and makes her sit on the bed. He sits next to her.

                    MOHAN
          (Softly)
     You took my phone to speak to someone
     yesterday because our landline was dead.
     Do you remember where you kept it?

                    MEERA
          (Meekly)
     I think... I didn't use it yesterday.

The doorbell rings. Meera tries to get up. Mohan makes her sit back down.

                    MOHAN
          (Sternly)
     You did. Now I want you to remember where you
     kept it while I get the door. All right?

Mohan walks out.

INT. MOHAN'S HOUSE — NIGHT.

CLOSE ANGLE of yellow lentils in a bowl. Anika takes a spoonful on her plate. Mohan eats with a napkin tied around his neck. Meera gets up to serve him more rice. Anika gestures her to sit down.

                    ANIKA
     Baba, where's your phone? Kishan called me
     a hundred times today.

                    MOHAN
     Ask your mother.

                    MEERA
     He can't find his phone.

                    MOHAN
     No! You must have kept it somewhere and then
     the maid must have stolen it.

                    ANIKA
     Don't talk nonsense, Baba. She has been
     working in our house for a year now.

                    MOHAN
     And I don't like her. She steals.

ANIKA
I've never seen her stealing. And if she wanted, she could have stolen my laptop or my phone. It's more expensive than yours.

MOHAN
Ani, you don't know anything. The other day she stole a packet of almonds. I got it from the market and it wasn't there the next day. Meera! Say something.

Anika is about to speak.

MEERA
Mohan, let it go. Ani, what did the carpenter say?

MOHAN
Why should I let it go? You listen to me.

ANIKA
Enough, Baba!

Turns to her mother.

ANIKA
He was suppose to give Kishan some drawings.

MOHAN
(Confused)
When did I mention drawings?

ANIKA
I don't know that. He said he called you.

MOHAN
He's lying. I didn't speak to him. Meera, did you pick up his call?

Meera frowns, tries to remember. CLOSE ANGLE ON ANIKA as she stares at her old parents.

ANIKA
Baba, no one's lying to you, calm down. It's been more than a week, please call him tomorrow.

MOHAN
I said I'll call him.

Mohan gets up, washes his hands and disappears in the bedroom.

INT. MOHAN'S HOUSE — DAY

Mohan vacantly stares at a teacup in his hand. Kishan sits opposite him with a drawing in his hand. INSERT of the drawing. Crooked and unsteady lines. He keeps it on the centre table.

                    KISHAN
        (Swallows)
    Chachaji! This will take time to make.

                    MOHAN
    I've all the time in the world. Take your time
    but make it exactly like this.

                    KISHAN
    One month minimum, *chachaji*. I'll have to go
    looking for these handles and doors.

                    MOHAN
    I'll come with you.

                    KISHAN
    It'll be too much for you. I mean... you're old.

                    MOHAN
    Who says I'm old? I can take care of myself.
    You tell me when, and I'll come with you.

Kishan nods meekly.

                    KISHAN
    Should I leave then?

                    MOHAN
    Yes. Take the drawing with you. Don't forget
    to call me.

Kishan shuts the door behind him.

EXT. OLD MARKET — DAY

A blazing sun scorches the tar road. The vendors and customers are going about their usual business. Mohan struggles to make his way through.

He walks on the same road as before, reaches the centre of a crossroads then slows down. Suddenly, he's not sure of where he is.

TIGHT CLOSE-UP OF MOHAN

THE DEPTH OF FIELD becomes very shallow, completely isolating him from his surroundings. He looks from one building to the other — from one person to another. His breathing quickens. He ventures a few paces in one direction and enters a small lane.

His face is flushed with fear. He sits down on steps in front of a shop and puts his head down, forcing himself to focus.

He sees someone waving at him but doesn't recognise them. CLOSE-UP of Mohan staring blankly in the camera. Ticking of the timer FADES IN.

INTERCUT — INT. CLINIC / MOHAN'S HOUSE — DUSK

Mohan stares in the camera blankly. TICKING of the timer continues. Muffled voices can be heard.

> DR DIXIT
> Are you with me, Mohan?

Pause.

> DR DIXIT
> Mohan, are you with me?

Normality returns. Everything is in focus now.

> MOHAN
> Sorry... Yeah... I'm...

> DR DIXIT
> It happens. Should we continue?

Mohan nods. The doctor pushes forward a glass of water. He refuses.

> DR DIXIT
> So tell me, what's your birthday month?

> MOHAN
> October.

> DR DIXIT
> Good. Where do you stay?

> MOHAN
> (Fumbles)
> A... a... Dadar.

INTERCUT

A truck moves into frame. PULL BACK to reveal the name 'Vasantkunj, Dadar' embossed on a marble tile outside a small bungalow. Kishan gets down from the front seat.

A FEW CREWMEN jump down from the back and start unloading the cupboard wrapped in a white sheet. Anika watches them standing at the door frame.

INTERCUT

> DR DIXIT
> Where in Dadar?

Pause. No response.

> DR DIXIT
> No problem. What is the date today?

                    MOHAN
            December... 15th maybe?

                    DR DIXIT
            It's January 15th. What is your wife's name?

Mohan is blank. He frowns. Tries to remember.

                    DR DIXIT
            Can you remember your wife's name?

Mohan looks at Meera. She gently strokes his hand and smiles warmly.

                                                    INTERCUT

A nameplate 'Meera, Mohan and Anika' is knocked off by one of the crewmen, trying to fit the cupboard through the door.

Anika picks up the nameplate, there is a scratch on Meera's name, she wipes it but it stays.

Kishan and the crewmen try different angles to fit the cupboard through the door. Anika watches them and smiles to herself.

                                                    INTERCUT

                    DR DIXIT
            No problem. Do you remember where were you
            before this? What were you doing?

Mohan is blank. He looks at the same objects, a pencil, notepad, posters and then at Meera.

                    DR DIXIT
            Do you remember anything about the cupboard?

Meera stares anxiously at Mohan.

                    MEERA
            Mohan, do you remember the Victorian-style
            cupboard you were making? With Kishan?

Mohan shuts his eyes, trying to remember. Dr Dixit and Meera exchange looks.
He opens his eyes, red and watery.

                                                    INTERCUT

A TIGHT CLOSE-UP OF ANIKA'S EYES — A tear rolls down her cheek.

She wipes her tears, turns off the gas and pours tea into five cups. We follow her into the bedroom.

The cupboard is set. Kishan removes the white sheet. Dust particles sparkle in the beam of sunlight.

Anika gives them tea and hands Kishan some money. Kishan hands her a dusty phone, screen cracked. He points behind the cupboard.

She stands in the balcony sipping her tea. Glances at the cupboard and then at the drawing in her hand. The cupboard looks exactly like it. She smiles. An auto rickshaw pulls up in front of the house.

Anika looks down. Mohan and Meera get out. She keeps the drawing on the wooden railing and walks out. A gentle wind blows, the paper turns. Another puff of air and it flies away, swaying tenderly.

FADE OUT.

JESSIE LOCKIE

Jessie Lockie is a scriptwriter from the South East. She is passionate about creating surrealist worlds and studying emotions. Surrounded by theatres, her love of writing flourished from the age of four. One of her plays was produced at the Stables Theatre and two short films produced by Drama Studio London. You can contact her at jessiemaryw@gmail.com.

MOULD
(a short film)

INT. APARTMENT — BEDROOM — MORNING

In a cluttered bedroom there is a mould stain on the ceiling. LILA (28), wearing pyjamas and fluffy socks, is lying on a messy bed.

It is raining outside the window. Outside we see a suburban street. The raindrops gather in a puddle on the windowsill.

There is a man, RYAN (30), dressed in jeans and a T-shirt, lying on the covers next to her.

                    LILA
I don't want to get up.

                    RYAN
You do, Lila. Get up.

                    LILA
    (exhausted)
Don't tell me what to do.

                    RYAN
I never do.

                    LILA
I don't want to go to work.

                    RYAN
It'll be fine when you're there.

                    LILA
Come with me, Ryan.

Pause.

                    RYAN
I wish I could.

The black mould stain has grown larger.

Lila stands up and walks into the living room.

INT. APARTMENT — LIVING ROOM

She walks past a table that is covered in bouquets of flowers.

CUT TO:

EXT. STREET — DAY

Lila puts her hands in her skirt pockets. She walks towards her work: a tall, grey office building. The rain is still pouring down. She looks up at the office. She is unable to go in and turns around to head home.

CUT TO:

INT. SUPERMARKET — DAY

Lila is putting food into her trolley and checking items off her list. Ryan is walking beside her.

                            LILA
            Peas... bread... milk... biscuits.

                            RYAN
            I thought you were eating healthily?

                            LILA
            I deserve them.

Ryan nods. She does deserve them.

                            LILA
            Olives.

                            RYAN
            Olives?

                            LILA
            Olives.

                            RYAN
            You don't like olives.

                            LILA
            You do.

                            RYAN
            Doesn't mean you have to buy them.

                            LILA
            Don't you want them?

                            RYAN
            Well, what do *you* want?

Lila shrugs and goes back to chucking food in her trolley.

> RYAN
> Think about yourself for a change.

CUT TO:

INT. APARTMENT — BEDROOM — EVENING

Lila cuddles a pillow as she watches a comedy. She doesn't laugh, she just blankly stares at the screen. She tries to eat an olive but grimaces and spits it out. Instead she stuffs handfuls of popcorn in her mouth, satisfied.

CUT TO:

INT. APARTMENT — BEDROOM — DAY

The mould on the ceiling is bigger now. Ryan is folding his clothes neatly and packing them into a plastic storage box.

Lila watches him from the bed, tears in her eyes.

> LILA
> Are you taking everything?

> RYAN
> Everything.

> LILA
> I want to keep something of yours.
> Just one thing.

> RYAN
> What?

Lila picks up one of his hoodies from the box.

> LILA
> This one. It was my favourite.

> RYAN
> No.

> LILA
> Ryan.

> RYAN
> No.

> LILA
> Please.

> RYAN
> And do what with it?

                              LILA
                    Wear it.

                              RYAN
                         (exasperated)
                    Wear your own clothes.

                              LILA
                    It smells like you.

                              RYAN
                    I know. But one day it won't and it'll take up
                    space.

Lila wraps herself in it and lies on the bed. He watches her for a while.
She doesn't acknowledge him. He goes to touch her, then pulls away.

Ryan places the box by the door and walks into the living room. Lila stares
at the box for a while.

                                                                    CUT TO:

INT. APARTMENT — BEDROOM — MORNING

Lila looks up at the mould. It is even bigger now. She picks up a cloth and scrubs
at it. It gets bigger. The box is still beside the door.

                                                                    CUT TO:

EXT. STREET — DAY

Lila walks to work. She stands outside, looking up at the building. She wipes her
eyes and walks inside.

                                                                    CUT TO:

INT. OFFICE — DAY

Lila walks past a sea of sympathetic faces and reaches her desk. On it is a card.
Her eyes blur.

                                                                    CUT TO:

INT. APARTMENT — LIVING ROOM — EVENING

Lila walks into the room. More flowers are on the table. Ryan is sitting in a chair.

                              RYAN
                    How was it?

                              LILA
                    OK.

                              RYAN
            Good?

                              LILA
            No. Just OK.

                              RYAN
            You'll go again?

                              LILA
            Yes.
Silence.

                              RYAN
            Come to see me.

                              LILA
            Where?

                              RYAN
            My new home.

                              LILA
            I don't think I want to.

                              RYAN
            You have to. For me.

                              LILA
            I don't think—

                              RYAN
            Please. Tomorrow.

                              LILA
            Will you be there?

                              RYAN
            I'm anywhere you want me to be.

                                                            CUT TO:

INT. APARTMENT — LIVING ROOM — DAY

Lila takes one of the bouquets of flowers from the table and leaves the house.

                                                            CUT TO:

EXT. CHURCHYARD — DAY

Lila walks through the graveyard, looking at a grave in the distance.
It says the name 'Ryan'.

She can't bring herself to walk over and turns to leave, dropping the flowers
on the ground as she goes.

CUT TO:

INT. STREET — DAY

Lila walks down the street purposefully. Ryan trails along beside her.

                    RYAN
Where are you going?

                    LILA
I'm going to replace the curtains.

                    RYAN
Do you really need to do that now?

                    LILA
What d'you mean?

                    RYAN
You have a meeting. With a therapist.

                    LILA
And I'm not going.

                    RYAN
You have to.

                    LILA
I don't. I don't need to at all.

An OLD WOMAN walking her dog goes past. She glances at Lila talking to herself and looks concerned.

                    RYAN
You need to talk to someone.

                    LILA
I don't. I have you.

                    RYAN
Yes, but—

                    LILA
You're the only person I need to talk to. You know me best. No use telling someone else about my day, is there?

Lila almost walks into a man, RICHARD (30).

                    LILA
Oh, sorry I... Richard! Hello.

                    RICHARD
Lila. It's been a while...

                    LILA
          Yes, it has.

There is an awkward moment between them. Richard doesn't know what to say.

                    RICHARD
          I heard about your... your husband.
          How are you doing?

                    LILA
          Oh. You know me. I'm fine.

                    RICHARD
          You're fine?

                    LILA
          Well, no. No. I'm not fine. But some days it's
          like he's still here. I feel him around me all
          the time.

Lila looks at Ryan, but he is gone. She tries to mask her surprise and upset.

                    RICHARD
          Listen, I'm on my way to work but I'd
          really like to catch up soon. For a drink
          or chat, maybe?

Lila is visibly shaken and looks around, not really listening.

                    LILA
          Maybe, yes. That would be great. I'll see you
          around. Bye.

Lila rushes off as Richard watches her go.

                                                              CUT TO:

INT. APARTMENT — LIVING ROOM — DAY

Lila careers into the room where Ryan is sitting in an armchair. She runs at him and falls onto her knees before him.

                    LILA
          Where did you go? You were there and then you
          just disappeared. You left me!

                    RYAN
          I didn't leave. I was there the whole time.

                    LILA
          You weren't. I couldn't see you.

Pause.

                              RYAN
                    I can't come out with you anymore.

                              LILA
          Why?

                              RYAN
                    It's not good for you.

Ryan gets up and walks out of the room. He is now more translucent.

                                                            CUT TO:

INT. APARTMENT — LIVING ROOM — EVENING

Lila sits in the living room with food wrappers and takeaway cartons all around her. It is clear she has not left the house in, perhaps, several weeks.

The phone rings. She waits for it to finish ringing and a voicemail is overheard.

                              RICHARD
                    Hello, It's Richard. Again. I don't think my
                    other messages have got through. I didn't
                    know what to say the other day, but I'm sorry.
                    You must be going through an awful lot. If
                    you got my messages and just don't want to
                    speak to me, this will be my last one. If you
                    didn't... Well, I'm sorry it was so awkward.
                    I'm not very good at these things. You seemed
                    freaked out. If there's anything I can do
                    to help, I'd be happy to. Please just let me
                    know. I'd still like to take you out for a
                    drink. That's it. Bye.

Lila sits there for a moment and then gets up and walks into the bedroom.

INT. APARTMENT — BEDROOM

Lila climbs into bed.

The mould now covers the entire ceiling. There is mess covering the floor and the bed. The sheets are wrinkled.

Ryan follows her into the bedroom.

                              RYAN
                    What are you doing?

                              LILA
                    Sorry?

                              RYAN
                    What are you doing? Sitting here?

                    LILA
          I'm sitting in my bed. Is that not allowed?

                    RYAN
          I mean here. In this flat. In this mess?
          What is this?

                    LILA
          I don't know what you mean?

                    RYAN
          This isn't you. I'm sorry, but it isn't.
          You don't sit indoors, ignoring the outside
          world, ignoring messages, not seeing anyone,
          not leaving the flat.

                    LILA
          I just don't want to go out. You can't
          make me.

                    RYAN
          You have to go out. You HAVE to.

                    LILA
          I don't have to. Stop it. Just stop it. You
          can't make me go out when I don't want to!

                    RYAN
          And why not?

                    LILA
          Because you're NOT HERE!

Lila shouts the last sentence, surprising herself. She bites her lip and tears fall down her cheeks.

Lila and Ryan are silent.

                    RYAN
          That's right. That's right. I'm not here.
          You should go for that drink with Richard.

                    LILA
          But you wouldn't want me to.

                    RYAN
          I don't want you to wait for someone who's
          not there, and to stay indoors every day.
          I want you to start living again.

                    LILA
          But I need you.

Lila tries to touch Ryan's hand with hers and presses her cheek to his. They are still.

CUT TO:

INT. APARTMENT — BEDROOM — DAY

Lila lies on her bed looking at Ryan's side which is empty. She closes her eyes for a moment and then gets out of bed and walks into the living room.

INT. APARTMENT — LIVING ROOM

She picks up the phone, dialling a number.

                         LILA
        Hey, Richard. It's Lila. I didn't get your
        messages. I'm sorry... Yes... I'd love to have
        a drink. A coffee. You can pick me up later...
        That's great... It'll be good to talk.
        See you later.

Lila walks through her flat, looking through each room. Ryan isn't there.

CUT TO:

INT. COFFEE SHOP — DAY

Lila sits in a coffee shop talking to Richard. He gazes at her from across the table. There is indecipherable chatter from all around the café. Every so often her eyes search around the room for Ryan but he is no longer there.

CUT TO:

INT. SUPERMARKET — DAY

Lila and Richard look for food on the shelves. She picks up a jar of olives and looks up at Richard. He grimaces. Lila puts them back on the shelf.

CUT TO:

INT. APARTMENT — BEDROOM — DAY

Richard scrubs at the mould on the ceiling with mould remover. Lila smiles from her bed. Ryan watches her from a smiling photograph on her bedside table.

CUT TO:

EXT. CHURCHYARD — DAY

Ryan's grave is in the rain. There is a bouquet of dying flowers close to it.

JAMES PICKTHALL

James Pickthall is an award-winning writer, composer, director and baker from Plymouth. He completed his Bachelor's at the University of East Anglia, where he continued his studies into his current Master's. His work has been performed at the Royal Academy of Dramatic Arts, the University of Westminster and Drama Studio London.

ENTROPY
(a radio play)

SCENE ONE

> INT. BEDROOM. WEST LONDON — DAY
>
> A HOT MAY MORNING. THE BEDROOM HAS AN EN SUITE. SILENCE FROM OUTSIDE. RB (24) AND WILL (25) ASLEEP IN BED. A LOUD PHONE ALARM ON THE FLOOR WAKES WILL. HE LEANS DOWN AND MUTES THE ALARM. HE TWISTS AROUND, SHAKES RB GENTLY.

WILL: RB. Wakey-wakey.

> **RB MOANS.**

Come on, time to get up.

> **RB MOANS AGAIN. WILL GETS OUT OF BED; BARE FEET ON FLOOR. LEAVES INTO THE BATHROOM.**

RB: (*close*) Whasgoinon? (*yawns, slightly louder*) What time is it?

WILL: (*off*) Five in the AM. Time to get up.

RB: What'd you just say? Will. What's going on?

WILL: No time to explain.

> **THE TOILET FLUSHES; WILL RETURNS, STARTS GETTING DRESSED.**

RB: Will, seriously, what's going on? Are we in the middle of a geopolitical crisis?

WILL: The only thing we're in the middle of is summer.

> **RB SITS UP. WILL PICKS UP A RUCKSACK BY THE DOOR, MOVES BACK TO RB.**

RB: This a joke? I don't do surprises.

WILL: (*close*) Listen. Pick out two articles of clothing, a towel, and meet me in the car in five minutes. I'll explain everything. By the way. Happy one-year anniversary.

HE KISSES HIM AND LEAVES. RB SIGHS, GETTING OUT OF BED.

FADE.

SCENE TWO

EXT. STREET. WEST LONDON – MORNING

OUTSIDE ELLIE (28) AND IAN'S (26) HOUSE. SAME TIME, BUT ANOTHER PART OF WEST LONDON. BIRDSONG. ELLIE RUNS FROM THE HOUSE TO THE CAR, THROWS A BAG INTO THE BOOT, AND CLOSES IT QUIETLY. THE SOUND ECHOES.

ELLIE: (*whisper shouting*) Come on!

FROM THE HOUSE, IAN CARRYING A BAG.

IAN: (*off*) I'm coming as fast as I can!

ELLIE: Shhh!

SHE RUNS UP TO IAN, TAKES THE BAG.

Give it to me, Ian. Your arm isn't broken anymore, you're not immobile.

IAN: Well, who was it, Ellie, who ran me over with her bike?

ELLIE: Just start the car. Got to go before the Saturday morning rush. Have you got everything?

IAN: (*moving away*) Yes, everything.

ELLIE STARTS LOCKING THE DOOR. IAN STRUGGLES TO GET INTO THE CAR.

ELLIE: All right, Ian. You're in charge, now. I'm not saying anything, you're calling the shots.

> IAN TRIGGERS THE ALARM; ELLIE JUMPS, RUSHES OVER.
> IAN TURNS ALARM OFF.

IAN: Now, look, you can hardly blame that entirely on me...

ELLIE: Let's just make it to the coast in one piece, shall we?

> SHE GETS INTO THE PASSENGER SEAT, PUTS SEATBELT ON.

... Numbskull.

> CLOSES THE DOOR. IAN TURNS THE ENGINE ON. AFTER A MOMENT, PULLS ONTO THE ROAD AND DRIVES AWAY.
>
> FADE.

SCENE THREE

> INT. WILL'S CAR – MORNING
>
> MUSIC: *WASHIN' AND WONDERIN'* BY STROKE 9 ON RADIO. WILL QUIETLY SINGS ALONG. SOMEWHERE ALONG THE M25. SOFTENED CAR ENGINE, VERY LITTLE TRAFFIC. RB FIDGETS IN HIS SEAT.

RB: Look, we're out of London, can you please tell me what's going on?

WILL: And ruin all this dramatic tension? Perhaps I should tell you in instalments?

RB: Will...

> BEAT. WILL PAUSES MUSIC.

WILL: All right. You've been saying recently, how you don't want the summer to end before we had time to enjoy it. Especially with our first anniversary coming up. So, last night, I started thinking.

RB: Thinking?

WILL: Thinking, as in, online research. I started looking for the best place a gay couple can spend a weekend, enjoy the weather, and be themselves. And I found somewhere.

RB: Where?

WILL: Dorset.

RB: Dorset? Why not Brighton, at least it's closer?

WILL: Nah, we need the full seaside experience. A place we can feel liberated and free. Where we can ignore those stupid attitudes towards the human body and—

RB: Yeah, OK, exactly *where* in Dorset?

WILL: It's a nudist beach called Studland Bay.

RB: Wait — excuse me?

WILL: Two days of natural living, RB!

RB: This isn't a good idea.

WILL: How?

RB: Will, come on, I'm not... prepared. You — you do know what I mean, right?

BEAT.

WILL: No, I do. But. This will be good for you. I'm not trying to force you into this, it's just, it might be a way to get past these difficulties. There'll be loads of people there.

RB GROANS IN DISCOMFORT.

No one else will care. We never go swimming, never do the gym. Maybe once you soften your paranoia, we can finally do things other gay couples do.

RB: Telling me I have no confidence doesn't exactly fill me with confidence. You can't just tell someone who hates their body to get over it, Will.

WILL: I'm sorry. Genuinely.

RB: (*beat*) But. I'll play along. As long as you're aware of how uncomfortable I am about this, or else—

WILL: No — no 'or else', trust me. I wouldn't put our relationship on the line for that. I'm here to help.

WILL PLAYS THE MUSIC AGAIN.

RB:	(*low*) Why do I doubt that?
WILL:	Hey, let's get some coffee; when's the next service station?

FADE.

SCENE FOUR

INT. STARBUCKS, FLEET SERVICE STATION – DAY

ELLIE ALONE, TEXTING. ECHOEY MUSIC. IAN ARRIVES, MUMBLING, WITH TWO TAKEAWAY COFFEE CUPS. HE PUTS THEM DOWN AT THE TABLE.

ELLIE:	Ah. (*sits up, slides cup closer*) See, wasn't hard, eh?
IAN:	Yeah, buying coffee *really* proves myself...
ELLIE:	Well, this is the only way you can prove to me your assertiveness. Ever since you broke your arm, all you've done is sit around feeling sorry for yourself.
IAN:	(*low*) WowyeahOK...
ELLIE:	However, today, I'm stepping back and letting you do everything. Drink your coffee.
IAN:	My problem isn't all that bad. I just need to get back into doing things normally. A day on the coast, that's all I need. It was your brother's boyfriend who suggested the coast.

IAN TAKES PHONE OUT, BEGINS TYPING.

ELLIE:	(*sipping coffee*) Will? Yeah, I like Will.
IAN:	We've been texting, so, just telling him what we're doing.
ELLIE:	What *you're* doing, Ian, today is your day. Even if it's a trip to the coast, it's still your decision. Drink your coffee.
IAN:	Yeah, I just need to find somewhere on the coast, first.

ELLIE: You still haven't — nope, sorry. I'm not interfering. You're in charge. (*sips coffee*) Will's nice. Good to see Ryan's found someone he trusts. (*beat*) You don't suppose he's ever told Will? I assume Ryan's, you know, over it? I don't think it's a problem, now. I'm open with people about it. I regret what I did, but—

IAN'S PHONE VIBRATES. HE READS THE NEW MESSAGE.

IAN: Oh, hey. Will and Ryan are going out for the day, too.

ELLIE: Where're they going this early?

IAN: Oh... I — I don't know, he doesn't say...

ELLIE: Probably Brighton. (*sips coffee*) Well, Ian? Ideas? What are you thinking?

IAN: Well... I *might* have an idea.

ELLIE: Tell me.

IAN: Once I've finished my coffee.

ELLIE: Well, hurry up and finish it, then!

IAN: It's still hot!

ELLIE: Then take the lid off the...

SHE STRETCHES ACROSS THE TABLE, TRIES TO REMOVE THE LID FROM IAN'S COFFEE CUP. HER HAND SLIPS, SPILLING HOT COFFEE ONTO IAN.

IAN: (*jumping up*) Ahhh!

ELLIE: Ian, stop it. At least that was an accident, this time.

IAN STRUGGLES WITH THE HEAT. ELLIE RISES, PICKS UP HER BAG AND COFFEE, AND GRABS IAN BY HIS ARM. THEY LEAVE.

Where're the toilets here?

FADE.

SCENE FIVE

> EXT. CARPARK, FLEET SERVICE STATION – DAY
>
> WILL, ALONE, TEXTING. A COACHLOAD OF RUGBY SUPPORTERS, COLLECTIVELY SINGING *IF I WERE THE MARRYING KIND*, ENTER THE SERVICE STATION.
>
> RB RUNS OUT.

RB: Good old rugby fans, eh?

WILL: Yeah. Your sister's boyfriend just messaged, they're out for the day, too. So, just explained where we're going.

RB: Oh no...

WILL: Look, they're probably going somewhere completely different.

RB: Will...

WILL: What's the problem? It's just you and me, it's fine.

RB: I'd rather not have my sister find out. I've already got enough baggage being torn open today.

WILL: Wait, your sister?

RB: Let's just get going...

> RB LEAVES. WILL SIGHS, FOLLOWS.
>
> FADE.

SCENE SIX

> INT. FLEET SERVICE STATION – DAY
>
> MOMENTS LATER. ELLIE, OUTSIDE OF TOILETS. HER PHONES RINGS; THE CHORUS TO *TOY* BY NETTA BARZILAI. IAN IS CALLING. SHE ANSWERS.

ELLIE: Ian? What's going on? I'm waiting outside the toilets.

IAN: (*distort*) Yeah. I'll be honest, I appear to have locked myself in the cubicle.

ELLIE: Oh my God, what?

IAN: Which is annoying, because I've just thought of where we're going. So, uh... little help?

ELLIE: Wait, where have you decided?

IAN: I want to keep it a surprise. Also, having to whisper slightly, there's people here now.

HE HOLDS PHONE OUT; RUGBY SUPPORTERS SINGING, AS BEFORE.

Can't quite make out what they're saying, but I think they might be an anti-establishment vigilante group.

ELLIE: Listen. If you tell me your plan, I'll get help. Either that, or you just get yourself out of the mess you've made. You're wanting to prove that you can make decisions. What's it to be?

IAN: (*beat*) Uh. How about... this be my 'get out of jail free' card?

SHE GROANS, HANGS UP, LEAVES TO GET ASSISTANCE.

FADE.

SCENE SEVEN

INT. WILL'S CAR — DAY

MUSIC: *LONELY BOY* BY ANDREW GOLD ON RADIO. SOMEWHERE ON THE M3.

WILL: Look. Why is your sister knowing what we're doing such a big deal? She's never been a problem up until now.

RB: Drop it, all right?

WILL: Maybe nudity might help you open up.

RB: Will, listen. Your heart is without a doubt in the right place but...

RB TURNS THE RADIO OFF.

...but this is pretty disturbing. There's something I'm missing, here. Tell me.

WILL: All right. I really wanted to try a nude beach. And I thought, with your self-image worries, trying to help you might be good... justification for going.

RB: Through forced exhibitionism?! That's monstrous.

WILL: Listen, we've only been together a year, you've never talked to me about your fears and—

RB: Oh, but, you're fine with exploiting them? Is that what this relationship's about?

WILL: Why not try and appreciate what I'm trying to do for you.

RB: I would if I could figure out what it is you're trying to do!

ENGINE BACKFIRE. WILL SLOWS DOWN, PULLS ONTO HARD SHOULDER. TURNS ENGINE OFF, HISSING.

Now what?

WILL: We need to check under the hood. Might have to call the AA. Maybe, I don't know. I need to... need to call...

WILL GETS OUT, SLAMS DOOR BEHIND HIM. RB RESTS HIS HEAD ON THE DASHBOARD.

RB: (*low*) Please just take me home...

FADE.

FIONA SANGSTER

Fiona Sangster is a television and film writer from Norfolk. She began writing scripts in 2016 after having short stories published in Germany, New York, and at UEA. This extract is the beginning of her MA dissertation, *The Organ Donor*, a six-part drama series. More info at: fionasangster.co.uk.

THE ORGAN DONOR

FADE IN.

INT. HARRISON'S FLAT — BEDROOM — EARLY MORNING

HARRISON YOUNG, 43, sprawls diagonally across a kingsize bed.

The walls are bare. There are some moving boxes in the corner.

He stares up at the ceiling, unblinking.

His alarm goes off: 5.30AM.

INT. BATHROOM — CONTINUOUS

Harrison brushes his teeth in the mirror, dead to the world. He is handsome in a middle-aged kind of way.

He spits in the sink — there is a little blood. He looks at his gums in the mirror: receding.

INT. BEDROOM — CONTINUOUS

He puts on black trousers and a white buttoned shirt.

He looks at himself in the mirror for a moment too long.

INT./EXT. HARRISON'S CAR — MOMENTS LATER

Harrison drives down a country road. He listens to (*I Can't Get No*) *Satisfaction* by The Rolling Stones on a CD.

He keeps checking his phone, almost hits another car.

Looks at himself in the rear-view.

EXT. NEW SCOTLAND YARD — MOMENTS LATER

Harrison approaches the building. He glances towards the collection of flowers and gifts that still stands in front of the building. A photo of Keith Palmer is in the centre.

INT. NEW SCOTLAND YARD — CONTINUOUS

The entrance hall is vast. There is little security.

He enters, flashes his badge to the man behind the desk, squeezes through a mechanical barrier, and gets in the lift.

INT. LIFT — CONTINUOUS

He presses '8'.

As the doors are closing, a hand comes in to stop them. In comes SANDRA CRESS, 46, stocky and hard with frizzy blonde hair.

The doors close in front of them as they stand.

                      SANDRA
Young.

                      HARRISON
Cress.

                      SANDRA
You ready for this?

                      HARRISON
Had my Weetabix and everything.

                      SANDRA
I hope those aren't your last words.

The doors pop open and the mood shifts. We are in a briefing room.

INT. BRIEFING ROOM — CONTINUOUS

It is solemn and silent. HENRIETTA MARR, 56, stands in front of a large projected image of a building layout. She wears a pencil skirt and flowered blouse, clearly not one for fieldwork.

In front of her are forty or fifty officers, sitting on tables, makeshift chairs, or standing.

Harrison and Sandra join the crowd at the back.

Henrietta checks her watch.

                      HENRIETTA
And that's seven. Hope everyone's here.
I won't repeat myself, so pay attention.

She takes out a laser pointer and, without humour, refers to the diagram.

                    HENRIETTA
     This is the headquarters of the gang that we
     believe have been providing the recent influx
     of cocaine to the lower Metropolitan area.
     One of our covert human intelligence sources
     has tipped us that

HENRIETTA   HARRISON
this is the location of   What's a covert
their distribution and   human intelligence
packing centre. There   source?
should be plenty of product

HENRIETTA   SANDRA
here so try and go after the   Snitch.
people packing it instead of
the product itself, there's
time for that later.

                    HENRIETTA
     Now. You'll get your orders from your
     captains. But I just want to wish everyone
     good luck. I know this will be a lot of your
     first time in the field with firearms but
     I want to assure you that you are trained
     for this. You could not be more prepared.
     Dismissed.

                    HARRISON
     What a load of shite.

INT. WEAPONS LOCK UP — LATER

Harrison signs his name and the date on a form. He slides it behind the counter and
is handed a pistol, an assault rifle, and a few magazines for each. He loads them
both, slapping the mags into place. He nods at the attendant and exits.

INT. POLICE VEHICLE — LATER

The back of a van. Harrison and others are geared up in bulletproof vests with
rifles. Their masks rest on their foreheads.

                    BEAT #1
     Mr Young? Have you killed anyone before?

                    HARRISON
     That's a bit personal.

                    BEAT #1
     Sorry, sir. I'm just nervous.

                    HARRISON
     It's OK to be nervous. Keeps you sharp.

                              BEAT #1
                    I used a taser on someone last week and it was
                    awful. He pissed himself.

                              BEAT #2
                    I had someone shit themselves before.

                              BEAT #3
                    That's nothing. I had someone do both.

They look to Harrison for his input to the conversation. Harrison sighs.

                              HARRISON
                    I had a certain suspect... ejaculate at the
                    stimulation.

The beat cops laugh.

                              HARRISON
                    To be fair, I tasered him in the balls.

They laugh more. The tension is lifting.

The van stops.

                              HARRISON
                    Quiet now. I think we're here.

                              BEAT #1
                    But sir. Really. Have you killed anyone?

                              HARRISON
                         (beat)
                    Yes.
                              BEAT #1
                    How did it feel?

                              HARRISON
                         (long beat)
                    It didn't feel like anything.

The doors to the van open and sunlight streams in. Harrison squints.

EXT. COCAINE BUST — CONTINUOUS

The building is run down and graffitied — it is undoubtedly used for
something illegal.

Ten police vans and forty officers, some already in position on the right side
of the building.

                              HARRISON
                         (quiet shouting)
                    B team! On me!

Ten officers approach him.

With silent gestures, he motions for them to follow him left. The rest of the officers disperse with their captains.

They round the left side of the building. There is one entrance.

Harrison holds up his palm — wait.

They prepare the battering ram in front of the door.

There is a tense moment while they wait for the radio.

The young officers look at each other, nervous. They look to Harrison for reassurance.

Harrison is unreadable.

Suddenly —

                        RADIO
        GO GO GO!!

The battering ram shatters the door and they're running through into

INT. COCAINE BUST — CONTINUOUS

the warehouse where another officer is yelling

                        OFFICER
        THIS IS THE METROPOLITAN POLICE! STOP WHAT
        YOU'RE DOING AND PUT YOUR HANDS UP! WE HAVE
        WARRANTS FOR EVERYBODY'S ARREST!

The warehouse workers scatter; some stay where they are with their hands up; some try and run; some are already cuffed. There is cocaine EVERYWHERE.

                        HARRISON
        Come on, boys.

He leads the team down some stairs into the centre of the action where they are IMMEDIATELY charged at by a warehouse worker brandishing a bat and

BANG.

They're on the ground. Harrison lowers his gun.

He looks round to his team. They are all wide-eyed.

                        HARRISON
        On me.

He leads them round to the left, into an office-like room where there are three women, all with their hands up.

                        HARRISON
        Johnson, Miller, get these three cuffed.

Two officers peel off from the group while the rest exit the office, out of the building.

EXT. COCAINE BUST — CONTINUOUS

> Harrison
> Start looking around for runners. Get in your pairs.

Pairs split off from the group. Beat #1 is with Harrison and follows closely behind him, albeit using Harrison as a bit of a shield.

Guns out, they walk in a straight line away from the building, entering some dense trees. Harrison and Beat turn on their torches.

> HARRISON
> POLICE! COME OUT!

BANG.

Harrison gets behind a tree, looks down at himself. He's fine.

Looks to Beat #1. On the ground. Hidden behind a tree.

> HARRISON
> You all right?

No reply. Then —

> BEAT #1
> (in pain)
> Yeah.

> HARRISON
> You get a look at him?

> BEAT #1
> No.

Harrison looks round the cover. Another shot fires off close to his head, hacking off a piece of bark.

> HARRISON
> I'm gonna run across, you tell me where the shot comes from, OK?

> BEAT #1
> OK.

Harrison closes his eyes for a brief moment of peace, then runs ten metres to another tree, which he ducks behind for cover. Shots are fired.

> HARRISON
> Where?

                    BEAT #1
          He's on your 4! Behind cover! He's got a
          bulletproof vest!

Harrison peers round to the left. Sees a shape reloading behind the tree.

He jumps out, fires three rounds.

The figure drops.

                    BEAT #1
          Did you kill him??

                    HARRISON
          No. I got him in the chest. Should break
          a couple ribs.

He approaches with caution. Sees a gun lying in the leaves.

The SUSPECT (40s) is on the ground, wheezing, trying to pull off his bulletproof vest.

Harrison raises his gun and the man freezes.

                    HARRISON
          Hands up. It's over.

The man puts his hands up.

                    SUSPECT
          OK! OK.

Harrison starts to cuff him.

                    MAN
          I think you punctured my lung.

                    HARRISON
          You know, I would have been within my rights
          to kill you, so count yourself lucky. Now,
          you do not have to say anything. But, it may
          harm your defence if you do not mention when
          questioned something which you later rely on
          in court. Anything you do say may be given
          in evidence.

His words fade out as we

                                                          FADE TO:

INT. NEW SCOTLAND YARD — BRIEFING ROOM — NEXT DAY

Henrietta leads a briefing. There are fewer officers present than previously. Harrison stands at the back, an observer.

                    HENRIETTA
          Three of the eighteen people captured have
          already told us the locations of their higher
          ups, and their information all matches.
          This has been a very successful operation,
          undoubtedly impossible without the effort
          of everyone here.

Henrietta makes eye contact with Harrison. She smiles. It's obvious she doesn't do this very often, but it's not unattractive.

There is a smattering of applause. Harrison joins in, hopeful.

The crowd disperses. Sandra comes and stands next to him.

                    SANDRA
          You did good, Young.

                    HARRISON
          Thanks, Old.

She smacks him on the arm.

                    SANDRA
          You coming to the drinks later? There must be
          forty blokes who wanna buy you a drink.

                    HARRISON
          Some other time. I've got plans.

He walks away. She just rolls her eyes.

INT. HARRISON'S FLAT — LIVING ROOM — THAT EVENING

There are more boxes. Nothing is unpacked except for a table, a sofa, and a framed photo of a young boy.

Harrison enters through the front door. Once inside, he leans back against it, takes a huge deep breath, and grins.

                    HARRISON
          Fuck yes.

He goes to his record player and pulls out *Let It Bleed* by the Rolling Stones. He sets it up. *Gimme Shelter* plays out.

He starts to dance to it. It's dad dancing, but he feels good.

He opens the fridge. The only thing in there is beer. He pulls one out and drinks deeply, before pulling out a pizza menu from a kitchen drawer.

Now he's singing along.

He dials the number for the takeaway. There is no dialling tone. He thinks nothing of it, throws the phone on the sofa, and keeps dancing.

He picks up another beer. Dances in front of the window.

His eyes are closed. He doesn't see the red dot on his chest.

The Rolling Stones song reaches its chorus.

BANG BANG.

The window smashes and he is thrown to the ground.

                                                                       CUT TO BLACK.

TITLES: THE ORGAN DONOR.

KATIE STOCKTON

Katie Stockton is a Welsh playwright and poet. She is interested in the themes of education, and cultural boundaries between England and Wales. Her plays have been produced seven times. Recently her feminist play was performed at the Maddermarket Theatre, and her critically acclaimed *Colloquium* produced at the UEA Drama Studio.

COLLOQUIUM

SCENE 1

Two Oxbridge entrance interviews conducted at once, or, these days, at any University deemed a 'Russell Group.' The dialogue jumps between the two duologues.

          PROFESSOR A
I've reviewed your application essays, and I am afraid to admit that they are perhaps a bit too academic.

          STUDENT A
(*Confused.*) This is Christ Church.

          PROFESSOR A
It is a matter I will endeavour to discuss with you during our time together.

          STUDENT A
Those essays were given impeccable marks from my teachers.

          PROFESSOR A
Ah, A levels. They do a good job of fogging up the windows.

          STUDENT A
My essays are too academic?

          PROFESSOR A
Well! That very much depends on what you define as academic.

          STUDENT A
I define? Well, of the academy.

          PROFESSOR A
Then yes.

          STUDENT A
My essays were too 'of the academy?' This being the academy.

          PROFESSOR A
Simply put.

A separate interview. STUDENT B is decidedly more smug than STUDENT A.

> **PROFESSOR B**
> I shouldn't be telling you this, but, you see, what we are looking for is a polymath. An interdisciplinary. Someone with their fingers in many proverbial pies.

> **STUDENT B**
> I act. I did a gold D of E?

> **PROFESSOR B**
> So be it.

> **STUDENT B**
> It was a three-day long expedition.

> **PROFESSOR B**
> Don't they tell you not to bring those sorts of things up before you get here? Listen. Do you know the dangers of education? Don't regurgitate.

> **STUDENT B**
> I'm sorry?

> **PROFESSOR A**
> Could you express to me the dangers of education?

> **STUDENT A**
> No, you said—

> **PROFESSOR A**
> Try not to regurgitate, please. 'Tis a waste of both our time.

> **STUDENT A**
> Uh — OK. The dangers of education are... being taught what to think, instead of how to think for—

> **PROFESSOR A**
> No, no, no! Do not regurgitate!

> **STUDENT A**
> I don't understand what you mean.

> **PROFESSOR A**
> Think for yourself! Answer for yourself. Do not regurgitate.

> **PROFESSOR B**
> And why do you want to study History?

> **STUDENT B**
> It's the study of the human condition. *La condition humaine.*

PROFESSOR B
Christ.

STUDENT A
Well, literature is the study of the human condition!

PROFESSOR A
(*Disappointed.*) I see. Of course it is.

STUDENT A
No, no, I am not being facetious. I _mean_ it.

PROFESSOR B
Would you rather be an apple or a banana?

PROFESSOR A
My father interviewed Tolkien. He gave the exact same answer as you all those years ago.

STUDENT A
And that's a bad thing?!

PROFESSOR B
Snog, marry, avoid: the Holocene, the Pleistocene, or the Anthropocene?

PROFESSOR A
Could God create a _woman_ he couldn't pick up?

PROFESSOR B
Snog, marry, avoid: the raven, the writing desk, and Lewis Carroll?

PROFESSOR A
Is the Pope Catholic?

PROFESSOR B
Right. If this chocolate biscuit was the existence of an absolute truth, would you risk it for a chocolate biscuit?

STUDENT B
I prefer custard creams. What does this have to do with history?

STUDENT A
I didn't know Tolkien said that, how could I?

PROFESSOR A
Osmosis, perhaps?

PROFESSOR B
I want to play a game with you. It's called twenty-one questions, you know the form, yes? Good. Except now, I am a historical event. Guess me.

STUDENT B
Aha! I bet you're the Holocaust? The big, unguessable, unquestionable event.

PROFESSOR B
No, boy. I am not the sodding Holocaust. Now, guess, please, properly.

PROFESSOR A
See, what we want to know is, are you teachable?

PROFESSOR B
I want to see how you get to me. What questions will you choose. Let's do ten, not twenty-one. Yes or no only, remember.

STUDENT A
I have learned everything thrown at me so far. In my coursework I got 96%...

PROFESSOR A
So you are learnable. But are you teachable?

STUDENT A
... I am not completely sure what you mean.

STUDENT B
Are you Before Christ?

PROFESSOR B
(*Looking Student B up and down.*) No.

PROFESSOR A
Your essays, they're high markers. So you can learn. But can you be taught? Do you see? Do you see the difference?

STUDENT B
Did you happen in Europe?

PROFESSOR B
Somewhat.

STUDENT B
Were you a battle?

PROFESSOR B
Somewhat.

STUDENT B
Did you involve kings?

PROFESSOR B
Somewhat.

STUDENT B
Professor! Are you trying to trick me?

PROFESSOR B
No. Five questions left. Be creative.

STUDENT A
About the human condition, sir, professor, I meant that. My answer to your question was true, it came from my heart. I did not learn it somewhere.

PROFESSOR A
An answer can never come from the heart, questions perhaps...

STUDENT A
No, no. I meant — I meant it, OK? And because of that, I cannot provide you with a different answer. No matter how much you provoke me.

STUDENT B
Europe, but not. Russia?

PROFESSOR B
No. Four questions left. What are you thinking about asking next?

STUDENT B
I want to narrow down the date.

PROFESSOR B
Yes?

STUDENT B
I want to ask before or after the Renaissance. Or perhaps the Industrial Revolution. That would show you I know a thing or two about defining moments in history. But I have only four questions left, so I need to go for something more precise. And not only that, professor, but a way of thinking that would appeal to you. (*Beat*.) Professor, you've let me cheat.

PROFESSOR B
I'm sorry?

STUDENT B
Your poker face. Either it needs work, or you just did that on purpose. You flinched on 'defining moments.' Which leads me to believe that you are the Fall of Constantinople. Am I correct? (*Beat*.) There wasn't much actual battling, you were more of a siege. You were in Europe and yet not, because Constantinople bridges the gap between what was Thrace and what is Turkey. Anatolia, they called it then. You involved kings and yet you didn't

because they called themselves Emperors and Sultans. And you reacted to 'defining moments' because you were one — once the Ottomans had successfully invaded Constantinople, the Portuguese had to find a new trade route to India, to avoid the unfriendly Ottomans. No more Silk Road. And then they accidentally found the Caribbean, and the New World in general. For many historians, it was the end of the Medieval Era. A turning point.

PROFESSOR B
First class.

STUDENT B
But you let me cheat. You signalled. That can't have been an accident.

PROFESSOR B
Perhaps it wasn't.

STUDENT B
I knew it! You think this game can't be won. History is too fucking broad, is that it?

STUDENT A
You want me to play, but I won't.

STUDENT B
I could have won, professor, I could do it.

PROFESSOR B
That would be a Herculean task.

PROFESSOR A
Snog, marry, avoid: the father, the son and the holy spirit?

STUDENT B
I thought you were going to play hard to get. But you gave it away. I feel as though someone just told me Santa isn't real. So much for the infamous Oxbridge interview.

PROFESSOR B
I am sorry to disappoint you.

PROFESSOR A
Are you familiar with Aristotle?

STUDENT A
Do bears shit in the woods?

PROFESSOR A
Language!

STUDENT A
Define?

PROFESSOR A
Don't be glib. Are you <u>acquainted</u> with his theory of active reasoning?

STUDENT A
Not completely.

PROFESSOR A
Then let's see if I can't teach you. Aristotle defined a dichotomy between active reasoning and passive reasoning. Active reasoning is based on decision making. Passive reasoning is based on instinct. Active reasoning is what determines human intelligence from animals. Aristotle said that slaves did not possess active reasoning, hence why they were enslaved. If a slave could actively reason, he would be able to liberate himself. OK? Do me a favour. Ask me why I want to study English Literature?

STUDENT A
(*Swallowing contempt*) ... Why do you want to study English Literature?

PROFESSOR A
Me? Well. I am interested in what is defined as literature. We have pieces that are definitely literary, yes? Like Shakespeare. Like *Hamlet*. And then we have pieces that are definitely not, like the Yellow Pages. But then we have those bits in between: poems in Hallmark cards, the Harry Potter series, Slam Poetry, Instagram Poetry, rap music, *House of Cards*. I want to be around people who are making the rules — finding out how we define these terms. What makes us decide what side of the fence these things land on. (*Beat.*) Are you happy with my answer?

STUDENT A
Am I interviewing you now, then?

PROFESSOR A
Well, that very much depends on what you define as an interview.

STUDENT A
It was a fine answer.

PROFESSOR A
And if I presented you your answer and my answer next to each other, and I asked you to determine which one involved passive

thinking, and which one involved active
thinking, which one would you pick?

> STUDENT B

Did I question correctly, then?

> PROFESSOR B

You have an impressive wealth of historical
knowledge, it would seem. But you're right,
I gave it away.

> STUDENT B

I wanted to play the game to the end of
its line.

> PROFESSOR B

You did. You did. You just don't realise how,
yet. Life isn't always about answers, hey?
It's the getting to them. That's where the
meat is. Welcome to Christ Church.

> STUDENT A

Do you liken most of your applicants
to slaves?

> PROFESSOR A

If I don't like the way they think.

> STUDENT A

You want me to prove I'm not yoked by my own
learning. But that is my honest answer. The
human condition. How am I meant to tell if
that has been given to me or whether it has
come from some inherent thinking process
I have been gifted with. (*Changing mental
direction.*) I once heard of a professor of
biology who walked in with some roadkill,
plonked it on the table, and asked a
candidate to simply 'analyse.' Am I the
roadkill here?

> PROFESSOR A

I'd never heard that one.

> STUDENT A

Do you toss these stories around with your
professor friends? This shouldn't be a game
to you.

STUDENT A stops. Looks at PROFESSOR A defiantly and stands on the chair.

> PROFESSOR A

What on earth are you doing?

> STUDENT A

Well, I don't fucking know, do I? You've
stripped me of all sense! Don't know myself!

                    PROFESSOR A
Get down.

                    STUDENT A
No.

                    PROFESSOR A
Why?

                    STUDENT A
I don't know.

They stare at each other incredulously.

                    PROFESSOR A
Durham would be happy to have you.

                    STUDENT A
You patronising fuck.

                    PROFESSOR A
Good day.

End of scene.